INDIA AND THE SIMON REPORT

INDIA AND THE SIMON REPORT

C. F. ANDREWS

GYAN

Published by

GYAN

Gyan Publishing House
5, Ansari Road
Daryaganj, New Delhi-110002
Phone: 011-47034999, 9811692060
E-mail: books@gyanbooks.com

Distribution Network
gyanbooks.com
India, USA, Canada, UK, Australia

ISBN: 978-93-7014-090-5 (HB)

First Published, 1930

2nd Impression 2025

Printed at: Gyan Press, Delhi.

INDIA AND THE SIMON REPORT
Author: C. F. ANDREWS

INDIA AND THE SIMON REPORT

By

C. F. ANDREWS

1930

DEDICATED

WITH GRATITUDE AND AFFECTION

TO

HORACE AND OLIVE ALEXANDER

PREFACE

This book is not intended to deal with the technical political details of the Simon Report, but rather to consider the causes of the resentment in India to-day against Great Britain which have led up to the present deadlock. For this resentment exists very widely among the educated classes, and it is growing deeper. The Commissioners have done painstaking work, but they have failed to meet Indian public opinion on its most sensitive side. The main reason for this lies in their not clearly appreciating what the National Movement has already accomplished under the inspiration of Mahatma Gandhi. For the awakening of the masses under his leadership has brought about a new India which is seeking by its own inner urge to find self-expression. It can never be forced back into an outworn and discarded mould. To fail to deal adequately with such a national upheaval as this, affecting millions of human lives, is almost like acting the play of *Hamlet* with the character of Hamlet left out. For, now at last, this new force is coming in like a flood, not only in India but all over Asia; and those who fail to reckon with it are like children building castles on the sand which will be washed away by the next tide.

During the last twelve years of the history of modern India, Mahatma Gandhi has been by far the greatest personality dominating the situation. In his political ideas he is the strange figure of a moral revolutionary essentially non-violent in character. By his own temperament and imaginative outlook he is peculiarly conservative. He idealizes the past rather than the present. His whole heart is with the village folk, and he loves to call himself a farmer and weaver. His aim is the simplification of human existence rather than its development along new avenues opened up by the use of the machine. He will have nothing to do with the latter except for the fulfilment of the most primitive needs of weaving and ploughing.

His extraordinary power to move men cannot be understood without a realization of his supreme trust in God to inspire and guide every action that he takes. He is a man of faith and prayer, humbly dependent upon divine aid and seeking by divine grace to keep an inner heart of purity and love, unstained by sin. To find God and to be found by Him is the one goal that is set before him.

In many of these aspects he is poles apart from Lenin, with whom he has been compared as the awakener of a whole rural people and the creator of a new national being. The one remarkable likeness between them lies in their volcanic energy of personality surging up from the very depths of their nature with ever new creative urge. They have both been able to fashion millions of human lives according to their will. Sun Yat-Sen in China had the inner power to do the same, but not to the same degree. It is remarkable that the three "village" areas of the world—India, China, Russia—have each been remoulded by the revolutionary force of a great personality in one and the same generation. Such an event, on a scale so immense, has probably never happened in the history of the human race before. It reveals the greatness of the present epoch.

Man is truly spirit. It is the spirit that quickens. Mahatma Gandhi has been able to appeal directly to the living spirit in man. How this has happened in India will be shown in outline throughout the chapters which follow. During the greater part of his life he had ardently supported the British Government whether in India or in South Africa. He believed that it stood for racial equality and racial justice. Only after "Amritsar" was this faith shaken.[1] Even to-day, while non-co-operating with the British administration in India, he continues to pay high tribute to British personal character. Wherever he has felt the administration to be wrong he has fearlessly spoken out and also expressed his own convictions in action. For every Englishman he has a sincere regard. Towards individual English men and women he cherishes a very deep affection. He still numbers among them some of the truest friends he has in the world. It should not be impossible to come to terms with such a chivalrous lover of truth and non-violence.

In the light of what I have here tried to explain, the

[1] See Appendices I and III.

reason for the failure of the Simon Report becomes more clear. The Commissioners at one time came very near to the heart of reality in India. They even acknowledged the unifying power of the National Movement. But at the critical moment of decision, instead of looking forward far enough and wide enough to strengthen by their own recommendations all that was progressive, they turned their faces back towards reaction and division.

They saw quite clearly the evils which would follow, if they gave way to the insistent demands that were made for separate electorates. They realized fully the mischief of the arbitrary rule of the Indian Princes. They understood the selfish policy of the great landlords eager to keep their peasants in subjection. They watched how the tiny privileged body of Europeans was seeking to extend its own special privileges. All this must have sickened them at heart, just as it disgusts every thinking Indian patriot.

On the other side, they considered very anxiously indeed the new National Movement under the moral leadership of Mahatma Gandhi. The boycott annoyed and troubled them; for they had come out with very good intentions. But they did their utmost to overcome their irritation. In one very important respect, they were able to break through their reserve. For they expressed in their Report their warm admiration for the Women's Movement. Like a breath of fresh air, they felt its influence sweeping through the dark chambers of religious bigotry and outworn social custom. The Youth League, straining impetuously forward to take the path of open violence, if Mahatma Gandhi's influence were withdrawn, also attracted their attention. They saw its implications and how potent a force it might be for good if rightly directed.

Yet quite inevitably they turned aside. With the relentless urge of fate, they were driven from one fortified position after another, back for the most part to those vested interests which claimed their first attention. It would have required a political genius of the highest order, in such circumstances as these, to have been able, across all the intervening barriers, to grapple with the one salient fact, that in Mahatma Gandhi's personality alone was that spiritual alchemy to be found which could fuse the old with the new, the medieval with the modern, and thus lead to a united Nation.

What is needed in Great Britain, to help us out of our present mental confusion about India, is that we should try to feel from our own hearts what the Indian people, as a subject race, are feeling. We should put ourselves in their place, as the world of mankind all around takes new form and shape, and they themselves are forced to remain a "dependency" of Great Britain. We have to follow out to its conclusion the golden rule of life which teaches us to do to others as we would wish them to do to us. The more we try to take this attitude, the more clearly we shall see that to appeal any longer to a past convention of "dependence" is entirely out of the question. Wholeheartedly we must take our stand on their side in the cause of freedom. When put to this vital test, the Commission fails to satisfy enlightened Indian opinion.

Let me give two incidents which have revealed to me with a flash of light much of what Indians are feeling. When I was in Tokyo with Rabindranath Tagore, the Japanese newspapers attacked him as the "poet of a defeated nation". The words went to his heart with a stab of pain; but he rose above them and wrote *The Song of the Defeated.* In this poem he described his own Indian people as the Bride whom God woos in secret:

> My Master bids me sit at the wayside
> and sing the Song of the Defeated:
> For she is the Bride whom He woos in secret.

Such a song as this is not unlike the refrain of the Magnificat. But what a depth of suffering lies behind the words!

Another vivid memory is that of a conversation, some years ago, with Sir Tej Bahadur Sapru, who had served long and faithfully as a member of the Viceroy's Executive Council. When I met him in Allahabad, after his return from England, he was almost desperate in his pessimism. He had seen Lord Birkenhead, and the impression he had received was that Great Britain was determined still to hold India in subjection. After leaving England he had gone on to Turkey under Mustafa Kemal. When he spoke to me about Asia Minor, his eyes flashed. He had witnessed a miracle of transformation wrought by the joy of freedom. "Charlie," he said to me, "when will your country realize the wrong that she is doing to us by keeping our very *souls* in subjection?" That one word "souls", which he emphasized, made me wince as he used it.

I do not agree with him, as this book will show, in his pessimistic outlook. He had not fully realized, when he spoke to me some years ago, what a transformation was taking place owing to Mahatma Gandhi. He was still looking to the British administration to accomplish what it could never do. But he was right in his opinion that the continuance of the policy of subjection and dependence would only lead to disaster in the midst of a world that was being stirred to its depths all round by the impact of new spiritual forces.

We do not understand in our own country what it means for a highly sensitive, intellectual, and imaginative people to be held in such a dependent state as India is held in to-day. Even if we ourselves do not intend it, the fact that British rule is felt as a bondage is now evident. Release from this bondage there must be. In this connexion I would call special attention to the important statements made by Tagore and Gandhi which I have quoted in the Appendix.

Meanwhile another evil has been creeping insidiously forward with which the Commissioners have failed to deal boldly. It is on the racial side that my own anxieties have become greatest of all. For in the Colonies and Dominions a racial antagonism against Indians has steadily grown until it has become acute. What is more serious still, this race and colour prejudice, marking out Indians as inferiors, has reached Great Britain itself and has actually begun to infect our own social life here at the centre. The outward signs of this infection are still only faintly marked; and what I have said may be challenged by those who have not yet observed it. But if the noxious fever develops, not only abroad but at home, then I fear there will be much less hope of friendship with India in the future. For it is on this racial issue that the East is very rightly most sensitive of all: and India is the intellectual leader of Asia. The mind of India is turning away from caste and race distinctions to the one universal aspect of humanity. She will never endure at such a time to remain submissive as a subject nation and to be treated as racially inferior. Her whole soul revolts against such treatment, and her universal spirit will conquer.

Let me thank those Indian friends who have helped me most in fashioning within my own mind the thoughts contained in this book. First, and chief among these, I would remember one whom in India we love to call Gurudeva—the poet Rabindranath

Tagore. His heart is the largest, and his mind is the widest, that I have ever had the good fortune intimately to know in a life of much wandering and search. With him I would associate Mahatma Gandhi, and one whom I have never met, except in the spirit, Arabinda Ghose. I would add the name of one who has passed away—the dearest friend I ever had—Susil Kumar Rudra.

This book has been finished under the kindly roof of Mrs. Ellis and her daughter at Wrea Head, near Scarborough. In the outer world a wild storm has been raging at sea, but within this house there has been calm and peace. May the great minds of India give to us in this turbulent West some touch of their own inner peace.

I would thank, in conclusion, my friend, Basil Yeaxlee, for his valuable help in the final revision of this book.

C. F. ANDREWS

July 21, 1930

CONTENTS

		PAGE
PREFACE		9
A SHORT LIST OF COMMON INDIAN WORDS		21
INTRODUCTION		23
CHAPTER		
I.	LORD BIRKENHEAD AND THE SIMON COMMISSION	31
II.	THE NATIONAL UPHEAVAL	39
III.	MAHATMA GANDHI	51
IV.	THE NATIONAL PROGRAMME	65
V	A CHANGED MENTAL OUTLOOK	78
VI.	THE SHAME OF SUBJECTION	87
VII.	THE VICIOUS CIRCLE ENTERED	98
VIII.	THE VICIOUS CIRCLE BROKEN	111
IX.	THE OLD LIBERAL IDEAL	124
X.	THE NEW RACIAL FACTOR	135
XI.	EAST AND WEST	146

APPENDICES

I.	INTERVIEW WITH RABINDRANATH TAGORE	153
II.	TAGORE'S MESSAGE TO THE SOCIETY OF FRIENDS	159
III.	MAHATMA GANDHI'S LETTERS TO ENGLISHMEN	167
IV.	MAHATMA GANDHI'S LETTER TO THE VICEROY	176
V.	MAHADEV DESAI'S STORY	186
VI.	HAROLD LASKI ON THE REPORT	188
VII.	WALT WHITMAN'S POEM ON LOVE OF COMRADES	189
INDEX		190

A SHORT LIST OF COMMON INDIAN WORDS

Titles of Reverence and Respect

Word	*Meaning*
Mahatma	A title of Gandhi meaning "Great Soul"
Gurudeva	A title of Tagore meaning "Revered Teacher".
Srijut (Sjt)	A common title equivalent to "Esquire".

Terms Used in Passive Resistance

Ahimsa	Non-violence.
Satya	Truth.
Satyagraha	Truth-force or Soul-force.
Satyagrahi	One who practises Soul-force.

Mahatma Gandhi's Hand-spinning Movement

Charkha	The spinning-wheel.
Khaddar, Khadi	Home-spun cloth.

Terms Connected with the Political Struggle

Swadeshi	Belonging to one's own country.
Swaraj	Self-government or Independence.
Purna Swaraj	Complete Independence; often implying separation from Great Britain.
Panchayat	The normal village committee of five, duly appointed, which manages village affairs.

Indian Coinage

Rupee	One shilling and sixpence.
Lakh	Seven thousand five hundred pounds.
Crore	Seven hundred and fifty thousand pounds.

INTRODUCTION

We are living in very hard and critical times both in India and in Great Britain. In each country the aftermath of the European War has left its own evil debt of misery and want behind it which cannot be liquidated soon. The current of human life, like some river that has been silted up in one direction, has abruptly changed its course and begun to flow in a new and unexpected channel. It would be difficult to say which country has been affected most.

In Great Britain, the unemployment figures have gone mounting up, year after year, without any sign of abatement. All the various organized efforts of different governments in power have proved quite unable to prevent this. In the mining districts of South Wales and in the cotton manufacturing districts of Lancashire the distress caused by unemployment has been most acute; but it is also widespread in almost every part of England and Scotland. At last it has forced itself upon the minds of thoughtful people as one of the most alarming features of these post-war times, appearing to indicate a weakening of the whole economic structure of Great Britain in directions that may lead to disaster. No true lover of humanity can fail to appreciate the serious loss it would be to the world if those high resources of thrift and industry and integrity in business, which have hitherto upheld Great Britain's place as a peace-loving and progressive nation, were to show signs of permanent decline. Among the British people themselves the old vainglorious, boastful attitude of a bygone age has almost vanished and a chastened sense of inner suffering, hard to be borne, has begun to take its place.

During the same period wherein this change has been coming over Great Britain, the distress in India itself among the very poor has painfully deepened. This again has been due in the first instance to the after-effects of the World War. I have been living among the poor in that vast country for half a lifetime, and have seen in recent years this misery continually increasing. The prolonged agony of war shook the whole fabric of Indian village life as it did that of urban Britain. It has caused everywhere immense upheavals. Though in certain districts some temporary advantage was gained, owing to the shifting of current market values, nevertheless the sharp rise in prices, especially of cotton cloth, was immediately felt by the poor; and acute misery was caused which I witnessed with my own eyes. It needs to be remembered that many millions in India are constantly living very close to the starvation limit. If we include the women and children, these pitiably half-starved, half-clad people can hardly number fewer than fifty to sixty million souls. The mind becomes bewildered as it tries to realize in individual units such a degree of suffering as this. People in Great Britain, who are facing their own unemployment problems, need at the same time to show sympathy towards the Indian people, who have to bear the intolerable weight of their own poverty and suffering with an almost superhuman patience. For hitherto one of the greatest stumbling-blocks between the two countries has been the lack of sympathy and understanding. The newspaper Press on both sides has been partly to blame for this; but intelligent interest, along with a much wider and fuller exercise of imagination, could do much to overcome initial difficulties.

Perhaps the severest strain of all in India, since the war, has been experienced by the educated classes. The hard, grinding penury of their daily lives, utterly unrelieved and unrelievable, has to be witnessed in order to be appreciated. In spite of their education, whereon their families, living under the joint family system, had built such high hopes, there has seemed no possible means of obtaining suitable employment. To my own personal knowledge, within the area where I have been working, whole joint families have sunk to ruin during these post-war days owing to the impossibility of finding work. It would be quite beyond my power to describe adequately in writing the misery I have witnessed, and what I have here barely outlined is not based on hearsay evidence, but is the result of constant painful experience.

In the one household of mankind these two countries, India and Great Britain, have become to a very great extent wrapped up in each other's destinies, and therefore intimately interdependent. The delicate texture, which binds whole peoples together in a common unity, has at these two points of human contact become closely interwoven. How all this came about will be a matter for consideration later, but the fact of it is self-evident at the present time. Therefore there appears to me to be a paramount need for that which I have earnestly entreated, namely, a greater sympathy between these two peoples, who share together to-day a common lot of human suffering and have somehow to face the future with a new outlook.

There is an Eastern proverb which states that when great kings go to war it is the poor grass that is trampled underfoot by the armies of both sides. In the political struggle, which appears to be impending between India and Great Britain, and yet might even now be avoided if sympathy and understanding took the place of ignorance and strife, we are apt to leave out of our calculation the daily, hourly hardships of these poor working men and village people on whose labour we ourselves depend for our own sustenance. Humanity, though it includes many races, is fundamentally and essentially one body. The words of the apostle Paul help greatly, in difficult times like these, to bring our minds to a proper sense of proportion and to give them a right direction. "But now", he says, "there are many members, yet but one body. And the eye cannot say to the hand, I have no need of thee; nor again the head to the feet, I have no need of you. Nay, much more those members of the body which seem to be feeble are necessary. . . . And whether one member of the body suffer, all the members suffer with it; or one member be honoured, all the members rejoice with it."

In the criticism and discussion of certain features of the Simon Commission Report which will follow in this book my one desire throughout will be to keep before my own eyes and the eyes of my readers those numberless men and women, poor in this world's goods, but rich in faith, whose destinies will be decided during this coming political struggle. Anything approaching the conditions of war, by the use of armed troops to repress freedom, must be abhorrent to everyone in both countries, and yet we appear gradually drifting into something of that kind. To me personally the last few months, with their continual record of fresh imprisonments, have been filled with desperate longing that at the last hour the way of peace may be found and bloodshed may be avoided. It is possible for me to state humbly and sincerely, with perfect truth, that each country has become equally dear to me now that I have grown old. For although my birth and education were in Great Britain and I was taught from my boyhood to love my country with a passionate love and devotion, yet it is also true that by far the best and happiest part of my life has been spent in India, where I have been welcomed by

The present moment, therefore, is favourable for a reconsideration of the principles underlying the conflict between India and Great Britain, in order that if possible a solution may be found without further delay. For the great danger ahead which everyone is feeling to-day is lest, under the tremendous strain of events, violence may at last break out in an intensive form, and a guerilla warfare, with all the miseries of incessant shooting and bloodshed in every part of the country, may take the place of the present passive struggle.

"The kings of the Gentiles exercise lordship over them, and they that have authority over them are called Benefactors: but it shall not be so with you. But he that is greater among you let him be as the younger, and he that is chief as he that doth serve."

St. Luke xxii. 25

INDIA AND THE SIMON REPORT

CHAPTER I

LORD BIRKENHEAD AND THE SIMON COMMISSION

What has brought about the present strained state of affairs between India and Great Britain? How has it come to pass that, at the time when Great Britain is in a chastened mood, India has renewed her previous non-co-operation in a more intensive form?

The original facts were these. A Royal Commission, called the Statutory Commission, had to be appointed. Its duty was to recommend to the British Parliament what changes should be made in the Government of India. Lord Birkenhead, the Secretary of State for India, instead of appointing a mixed Commission, on which Indians and British should serve jointly under a British member of Parliament as Chairman, nominated a Commission of seven members drawn solely from the British race, without any Indian representation, even though it was the future Constitution of India which was to be the subject of inquiry. It meant that a purely British Commission should be the chief adviser of the British Parliament as to what the future constitution of India should be.

I know for certain that Lord Birkenhead was very

strongly warned beforehand against adopting this procedure, because it was certain to cause trouble in India. It would be regarded as racially insulting thus to ignore Indians when their own Constitution was at stake.

There was also another reason why it would give offence in India. For some years past it had been made a precedent that in every Commission dealing with Indian affairs Indians themselves should have full representation. In the Lee Commission and the Skeen Commission this had already been done. This was one way in which Indian self-government was already being forwarded simply and naturally; and it had led to the best results, restoring confidence in the good will of Great Britain.

It happened that just at the time of the appointment of the Simon Commission race feeling was running very high in the East. To ride rough-shod over national sentiment and appoint a purely British Commission on a subject so vitally and intimately affecting India was surely asking for trouble. It was bound to lead to disaster. But with an obstinacy that put on one side every warning offered and flouted Indian opinion, Lord Birkenhead carried through his own fixed purpose as Secretary of State and sent the Simon Commission to India without a single Indian member upon it.

Let it be made quite clear that there was not the least objection in India to Sir John Simon himself as Chairman. On the contrary, it was recognized by political leaders that a better choice could hardly have been made; and Indians would have been ready and willing to work under him. But they were not prepared to see their own Constitution reported on by British Commissioners alone, as though they themselves had nothing to do with it except in a subordinate way. It was freely said at the time that General Smuts and General Botha would never have been treated in that way when the constitution of South Africa was at stake; but because Lord Birkenhead regarded Indians as a racially inferior and subject people he was treating them in this manner.

The ostensible reason given by Lord Birkenhead for this wilful departure from precedent only made matters worse to sensitive minds in India. He stated that there were so many mutually hostile sections that it would be quite impossible to choose Indians without offending some of them, and therefore it would be better to leave them out altogether and let British representatives decide these important matters for them. This "rubbing-in" of Indian internal divisions, which has become especially common among British writers and politicians, was felt to be scarcely less humiliating than the racial discrimination itself. It was a thrust at India's own internal weakness that was undeserved.

In reply to Lord Birkenhead it was at once pointed out that in their own country Hindus and Muhammadans, men of the highest character and unimpeachable integrity, had already held side by side, with dignity, the chief positions in the State. There had been Indians, for instance, holding the office of Chief Justice, and an Indian had already been the Governor of a Province containing nearly fifty million people. There had been Indians—Musalmans and Hindus alike—who had been colleagues of the Viceroy on his Executive Council, acting as his intimate advisers side by side with Englishmen and Scotsmen. No question had ever been raised concerning their integrity, nor had there been any difficulty in their working together. On the contrary they had won universal regard from all sections of Indians and Europeans alike. In the same way, at the India Office itself there had been the long-standing precedent of Indian members serving on the Secretary of State's own Council. It was surely insulting to Lord Birkenhead's colleagues to say that no Indian could be found whom Indians themselves would trust as impartial.

One further argument was attributed at this time in India to Lord Birkenhead. He was said to have declared that it was necessary to choose only members of the British Parliament. But such an argument as this could hardly have been brought forward seriously, because there was nothing whatever in the Statute or in any previous precedent which would thus limit the choice of names; and even if there had been, Lord Sinha was at the time a member of the British Parliament. The question was naturally raised in India, why he at least was not chosen by Lord Birkenhead and thus this invidious exclusion of any Indian member avoided. For Lord Sinha's past record was second to none for service rendered. He had already been for many years a distinguished and honoured member of the British Parliament, sitting in the House of Lords. In this position he had been appointed Under-Secretary of State for India, and had been a member of the War Cabinet and of the Imperial Conference. In India he had served on the Viceroy's Executive Council, and he had also been the Governor of Behar and Orissa. In both India and England he was recognized as an outstanding figure because of his integrity of character and commanding intellectual ability. In addition to this, he was acceptable to Indians on religious grounds, because, as an earnest member of the reform movement called the Brahmo Samaj, he stood above sectarian divisions. If chosen as one of the Commissioners, there could be no doubt at all that he would loyally help the Chairman and his colleagues to the very best of his power.

But Lord Birkenhead selected, on purely racial lines, what was immediately called in India a "white" Commission. In a later chapter I shall endeavour briefly to describe how the evil of colour prejudice has become virulent as a disease in British India, and how racial arrogance has been at the root of most of the mischief between the two peoples. To display, therefore, a cynical indifference to Indian sentiment, to take no notice of this factor in a situation requiring the most delicate handling, to persist, against all advice to the contrary, in bringing the racial and colour issue into the selection of the Commission itself—to do this casually and lightly was a gesture of overbearing wilfulness which is hard to forgive. If it was done in sheer ignorance the action is hardly less to be condemned. For it shows that a man who could commit it was utterly unfit by temperament to be Secretary of State for India. It also reveals, like a flash of light on a dark picture, what a precarious position the people of India are in, if they are dependent every moment, with regard to things vitally affecting their future, upon the whim of a Cabinet Minister at Whitehall, seven thousand miles distant, who has never even visited the country. The result of Lord Birkenhead's act has been to leave behind an altogether unnecessary atmosphere of mistrust and resentment.

It was also, if one only thinks honestly about it, a gross injustice. For it is essentially an unjust thing to refuse to offer to eminent Indians themselves a share in drawing up a Report about the future government of their own country. This may be most easily shown in the following manner. Suppose, for a moment, that the words "India" and "Great Britain" were reversed, and that Indians were appointed to draw up a Report concerning the future government of Great Britain. Would Great Britain ever consent to an Indian Commission, however wise and learned, reporting upon the framework of a new British Constitution without any British representative as a colleague? Surely the British people would demand that they should frame their own constitution. And if we claim this right for ourselves, why should we not accord the same right to others?

It has been necessary to labour the point because it is just here where the shoe pinches. Rightly or wrongly, it was felt all over India that Lord Birkenhead's act in this vital matter was that of a conqueror imposing his will upon a conquered and subject people. It was in no sense democratic. It was like a racial superior acting with arrogance towards a racial inferior. That, at least, was how it appeared to every sensitive Indian who thought at all about it. It made no difference that professions of equality were offered afterwards, and devices formed for holding what were called "free conferences". The Simon Commission itself remained entirely exclusive in its own membership. The initial blunder continued with all its mischief.

There was another incident which drove the resentment still deeper. The fact that the Labour Party had agreed with Lord Birkenhead that Labour Members of Parliament should serve on a Commission of this unfair and racial character gave to enlightened public opinion in India a very grave shock indeed. Lord Birkenhead's nature and reputation were well known; but it could hardly be credited that the British Labour Party, along with the Liberals, would give open sanction and support to Lord Birkenhead's policy. For this reason the news came as a shock to politically minded Indians. It has led to a lack of confidence in the professions of the Labour and Liberal parties ever since.

When the Commissioners at last set out for India they found a difficult atmosphere awaiting them. The Report makes only very slight reference to this, in guarded language. But the facts were evident on every side. In spite of the news which the daily papers in Great Britain used to recapitulate week after week, telling about the wonderful success of the Commission in breaking down opposition, the real truth was that, by failing to secure the co-operation even of the moderate Liberal group in Indian politics, who had stood beside the British Government all through the earlier non-co-operation movement, the Simon Commission never had a chance of success. The very persons who could have given the Commission the wisest counsel if they had been members of it stood apart on principle and refused to co-operate with it. There could hardly have been a more severe condemnation of Lord Birkenhead's policy than this.

CHAPTER II

THE NATIONAL UPHEAVAL

The painstaking industry of the Simon Commissioners and their staff of workers is worthy of great commendation. The external facts of India are presented in a lucid and informative manner, and in certain chapters, such as those on Local Self-Government and Education, in Volume I, it is evident that they had expert advice and counsel which was both sympathetic towards Indian aspirations and critical of the present system. There is also throughout a courtesy of tone towards Indians generally that makes the Report a welcome change from the cold attitude towards the human side of life which Blue Books often represent. Immense pains have been taken to avoid the assumption of a dominating racial attitude. All this and much more might be said concerning the Report in certain important directions. Personally I have endeavoured in all that I have written, even though I have differed radically from many of the conclusions, to give the Commissioners every credit for good intentions and to lay stress on the positive and constructive side of their work, accomplished under difficulties for which they themselves were hardly responsible. While making this as clear as possible, it is necessary at the same time to add that the Report has been to me, on the whole, the more I have studied its details and considered its main conclusions, a very disappointing document.

The reason for this disappointment is that there appears to be something lacking which throws the whole picture of modern India out of its true perspective. It deals much more with that old India which I knew when I first went out nearly thirty years ago, before the National Movement had started; it shows little understanding of the Young India which we see rising to-day on the tide of national upheaval. This India is almost strange compared with the old. Nothing less than an inner revolution has occurred. One of the ablest Englishmen who was intimately acquainted with the village life of India said to me that after coming back from a short furlough he had felt very strangely out of touch. We all feel it; and I know well that if I were to go back at this moment I should have to revise many of my old mental pictures.

Since the Report is to make recommendations for the future, this lack of true vision of Young India is a very serious affair. For it is clearly this India, and not the India of thirty years ago, to which the future belongs. The Commissioners have failed, not from any want of courtesy, but because they have hardly come into close contact with the people at first hand.

A very simple analogy may illustrate my point. New Delhi has been built by British architects at enormous cost to the Indian public. A slight attempt has been made by these British architects to put in here and there a touch of India; but the effect is altogether different from the indigenous architecture of the country. Even now it may be gathered from Indian experience and sentiment, already widely held, that the official buildings of New Delhi are unsuited for India. In the same way a political architecture, built up on a British model by seven British Commissioners, is likely to be equally unsuited to Indian conditions. The people of the country will not feel at home in it. Naturally they will prefer their own political structure. Only when they get what they want will they be satisfied.

A further parallel might be taken from the growth of the Indian Christian Church. Here again the missionaries have imposed their own Western scheme of things upon the constitution of the Church. The consequence of this has been that a revolt is taking place to-day among young Indian Christians because they cannot feel at home within the limitations which have been imposed by their missionary teachers from the West. There is exactly the same spirit of non-co-operation here that we find in the Indian national life. The cry of the Indian Church, as well as of the Indian nation, is for Swaraj. The Indian Christians desire an Eastern expression of Christianity wherein they can feel at home.

It is, of course, impossible for any single individual

to speak in general terms about the whole of India with any degree of accuracy. The area is so vast. But what I have personally witnessed, wherever I have gone, either in the extreme North or in the furthest South, has been a new national life breaking through the old shell of hard, encrusted social systems, creating in India a revolutionary element that is growing stronger in its opposition to foreign rule and in its determination to be independent. It takes many forms, and it varies, in different Provinces and among the diverse religious communities, in its intensity. But it bears one distinct characteristic. It is a movement of the spirit of man seeking freedom.

In the *Spectator* of July 26, 1930, a letter is published from an Englishman in Bombay who writes as follows:—

> "I am deeply impressed by the sincerity of the Indian leaders, and I am afraid people at home do not realize how strong feeling is—there is absolutely *no* antagonism to the English as such. My treatment by Indians of all schools here—even in a hot-bed of Gandhism—is perfect, but they claim the right to manage their own affairs. All the Hindus in Gujarat, from Gandhi down to the meanest member of the depressed classes, are solid in their demand; and in the twentieth century we cannot deny the right of self-determination to 320 million people. . . . I tell you in all solemnity

> that Indians are prepared to ruin themselves if necessary, in the same spirit that the Dutch flooded their own land in the fight for freedom. I never realized that the Indians were capable of such an effort. Men are not only cheerfully going to prison but are cheerfully allowing their lands to be confiscated in return for non-payment of taxes. When a country's spirit is like that, how can any real Englishman (who loves his own country and thinks what he would do if his own Motherland were in alien hands, however justly it were ruled) help but respect a people who are by nature pacific and non-violent. . . ."

The change which is thus graphically outlined from the field of action itself has come about with very great rapidity, as a revolutionary upheaval on peaceful lines. We cannot understand it aright unless we realize the unique personality of Mahatma Gandhi. It is extraordinarily difficult in prosaic modern England to give any conception of the emancipating influence of this romantic figure. We have to go back to the Middle Ages and study the effect of the Franciscan Movement on Western Europe. This analogy may startle some of my readers who do not know Gandhi the man, and do not understand what moral power he wields in India to-day. But I can say without any hesitation, as one who has studied modern India closely, that the analogy holds. I have lived in the midst of the revolution that Gandhi has inspired, and I have also lived at a distance from it and seen it in perspective. There is no question in my own mind as to what the verdict of history will be. The new life that has come to India through Gandhi has created the National Movement. But it is like no other national uprising in the world because its unchallenged leader has refused to appeal to force, and has suffered imprisonment time after time along with his followers. It is, in effect, a religious revolution, which has taken a national form.

Let it be remembered that Legend is still one of the most potent influences in the life of the Indian village people, who are spiritually alert and intellectually keen. The power of a religious personality, such as that of Mahatma Gandhi, on such simple and fresh intelligences is far greater than we in the modern West can imagine. We have to go back, therefore, to the Middle Ages for our examples, for those were rightly called Ages of Faith, in which miracles such as we witness in India to-day really happened. We all recognize that the Franciscan Movement changed the face of Western Europe and ushered in vast political changes. In the same way the Gandhi Movement is changing from within the face of modern India and creating a vast political upheaval. I cannot stop to prove this, but I do unhesitatingly affirm it as a definite concrete fact and not as a vague, sentimental belief. In the books I have written about Mahatma

Gandhi[1] the evidence for all that I have here briefly stated has been given in full.

It may be well, however, for the sake of those who would challenge these statements concerning his influence, to give some actual instances of his magnetic power in India. Once he had promised to speak at a very remote place in Gujarat on an evening in the dry cold weather, and the village people, as usual on such occasions, began to flock to the place from every side in their family bullock-carts, or else to come in on foot, walking twenty or thirty miles. For two or three days before the meeting the roads were thronged by this universal migration to see Gandhi. It was like the festival occasion of a great pilgrimage for all the village folk. That night there was an eclipse of the moon, and since the villagers were mainly Hindus they would naturally perform some religious ceremony at the exact time of the eclipse according to their ancient custom. The meeting was held in a large open space, and the villagers were sitting closely packed together in a vast circle. There were nearly as many women present as men. Indeed, it was a family exodus, for children were present also. The crowd was so dense that it was extremely difficult for us to make our way through without treading on someone.

During the time of the meeting the eclipse actually

[1] See, for instance, *Mahatma Gandhi's Ideas* and *Mahatma Gandhi: his own Story*, published by George Allen & Unwin Ltd., London.

took place, but the crowd was so absorbed in attending to Gandhi that no one moved. When I asked about this, a villager who was near to me said: "The *darshan* (religious sight) of Mahatma Gandhi is itself a ceremony of purification. What more is needed?"

Since I had to go away before the meeting was over, I was curious enough at the moment to count the number of steps that I took, very carefully and slowly, in order to get out of the crowd with the least disturbance possible. They were about one hundred and fifty in all. So this represented the radius of a huge circumference wherein the audience was very tightly packed. On a rough calculation, I put down the number present at about one hundred thousand. This would have been nothing unusual during the days of the non-co-operation movement of 1920–22. But no one except Gandhi himself could attract a crowd like that.

During the present upheaval I have been told that the concourse of villagers has been far greater than ever. There is an account about North Behar, which is on the opposite side of India to Gujarat. The statement was made in *Young India* that wherever Gandhi went in Behar it was estimated that the numbers of the crowd which came to meet him were more than double those who had come in the non-co-operation days. At one place it was reckoned by Mahatma Gandhi himself, who is very careful in such matters, that there were over two hundred thousand persons present. On this occasion so impossible was it for him to reach even a fraction of this vast multitude, in his tired state, by speaking aloud, that he determined instead to employ the dignity of silence. He sat in their midst in absolute quiet, without a word being said, and then went away. The crowd was quite satisfied. They had all seen Gandhi. They had received their *darshan*, and that was enough.

The greatest difficulty of all on these occasions, as I have very often experienced, is to prevent the rush of the crowd to touch his feet on his departure. He is very frail in body and small of stature. The crowd becomes so overwhelmed with a kind of religious ecstasy of devotion that it is almost impossible to control it. For days beforehand instructions have to be given throughout the villages that Mahatma Gandhi does not at all like this form of respect and devotion; but the difficulty of controlling a religiously emotional crowd remains. He himself has learnt by long experience to get through this trying ordeal with the greatest speed possible; but it has always remained a difficulty hard to overcome.

If it be asked whether this devotion is confined to Hindus, I would answer that in the main it is not. I have seen Muhammadan villagers, whose forefathers were Hindus and who possess the Hindu spirit of devotion in their own inner characters, coming to Mahatma Gandhi as a great saint.

Let me tell what happened in one of those parts of Behar that are very near to the foot-hills of the Himalayas and therefore not easily accessible. It was at the very beginning of the spread of his amazing influence and long before the non-co-operation movement. My own dress was in the Indian fashion. Throughout this northern part of India many of the people have a fair complexion. Therefore with my beard and Indian dress I passed for a time almost unnoticed. Then the news spread that I was travelling with Mahatma Gandhi. The crowd immediately gathered round me in a very friendly manner, and the one question that they wished to ask me was when they would get Swaraj, or self-government. It surprised me that the longing for Swaraj should have penetrated into such an extremely remote part of the country at such an early date. Since that happened much water has passed down the Ganges.

In Assam at the height of the non-co-operation movement Mahatma Gandhi's tour through the interior villages resulted, within six months, in a drop in the opium consumption by nearly twenty-five per cent., and the moral effect of his visit in this direction has continued ever since. Assam is no longer the "black spot" of India that it was in previous years. The opium addiction has never revived. The educated Assamese, who had not themselves suffered from the curse in the same way as the villagers, took up the moral issue, and they have done wonderful things. To those who know how almost incurable the opium habit is when it has got deep into the heart of the villages as it had done in Assam, the story of this change in the people's customs will appear almost incredible. But the dynamic force behind this was Gandhi's personality. And when one has seen it, as I have, doing its healing work, then we are obliged to think in other terms than those which are regarded as credible at ordinary times.

I will give another story that reveals how individual he is in his tenderness, as well as having at the same time a vast compassion for the multitude. An Indian Christian whom I knew had wished to come and see me while I was with Mahatma Gandhi at Juhu during his serious illness. The young man had just lost his mother, who had been for many years a widow, his father having died when he was quite young. Gandhi was still very ill, but the sorrow of this young Indian Christian deeply affected him. He would not let him go back until he had called him three or four times to his bedside to ask him to open his heart in his grief, and when at last he departed he said: "You must always consider me to be your father and Kasturbai (Mrs. Gandhi) your mother, and you have a place in my house as your own home." It was a very simple incident; but it represents a perpetual life of love and service which has been the secret of his influence with the poor.

The same Indian told me how on a later occasion he happened to mention to Mahatma Gandhi the pain he had suffered when a Hindu wearing a Gandhi cap had refused some water that he had offered in all kindness of heart. Early next morning, directly after the prayers at four o'clock, Mahatma Gandhi called him. He said that for the whole of that night he had not been able to get any sleep at all, because he had felt in his heart just what the Indian Christian had felt when his kindness was refused. He had been trying all night long to devise a remedy. For, he said, thus merely to keep the letter of orthodox Hinduism, while breaking the spirit, was against all true religion.

"I am just an ordinary human being," Gandhi said once in my hearing, "and full of weaknesses and sins. But I have this one thing that the poor recognize in me at once: they know that I share all their hardships. You could have the same influence, if you would do the same."

CHAPTER III

MAHATMA GANDHI

The question has been asked whether Mahatma Gandhi's influence is mainly political, or whether it is moral and social at the same time.

It is impossible to draw these sharp distinctions when one listens to his simple dramatic talks with the villagers. He is always practical, and never says a word too much. He is also a born teacher of simple, unsophisticated people. Let me take a typical instance, such as I have frequently witnessed. It may be that, when the village audience is very primitive and the crowd is immense, he will take his hand with its five fingers and its wrist. He will compare it to five branches coming out from the trunk of a tree, or some such parallel, and then he will begin his lesson.

The first finger, or branch, will stand for Hindu-Muslim unity. Hindus and Musalmans must learn to respect one another, because they are brothers and sisters. They must by no means quarrel over trifles or annoy their neighbours.

The second branch, or finger of the hand, will stand for the removal of "untouchability". No one must be an "outcaste" any longer. Every human being is sacred, and no single person must ever be treated as impure or unclean.

The middle finger stands for equality between man

and woman in God's sight. Man must treat woman as an equal. The whole purdah system must be abandoned, wherever it is still in force. The age of marriage must be raised. The ever growing evil of prostitution in the cities must be removed. He fearlessly faces the whole problem of sex relations on the basis of equality. At the same time he will have nothing to do with birth control, which he regards as contrary to the divine law of human existence.

The fourth branch, or finger, represents the prohibition of all liquor and drug-taking. He points to the crying evil of doping the little children with Government monopoly opium in Bombay. Such things must go, and the foreign spirituous liquors must not be imported They have brought ruin to India, and a clean sweep must be made of them. "*They* are the real 'untouchables'," says Gandhi. "No man or woman can pollute us by their presence, but opium and liquor can." Here he will pour scorn on the absurd social convention of refusing to touch a human being. The shrewd villagers smile and say to one another, "He is right."

The fifth and last finger on the hand represents the greatest innovation, namely the promotion of home spinning and home weaving in every village in India, so that the village families may spin and weave their own cloth out of the cotton that grows at their own doors instead of buying it. This work does not interfere with their agricultural labour, but rather supplements it. For it gives the villagers an industry, simple and inexpensive, to be followed in their spare time when it is impossible for them to cultivate the fields on account of the dryness of the soil. This *khaddar* (home-spun) programme is the most important economic fact of all. It saves the villagers from drifting into the towns when they are reduced to extreme poverty by lack of employment. The money that is now spent in buying cloth can be used for providing the family with more food. Thus the worst vicious circle of all is broken through by increasing the inner resources of the peasant and strengthening his moral character with a sense of self-dependence. Swaraj, says Gandhi, is first to be won within, and secondly in the family circle. Then it must be won in the whole village, which should be made sanitary and clean and free from jungle by the work of all the willing hands in the village, boys and girls included. This and nothing less is involved in Purna Swaraj (complete self-government).

After the five fingers have thus been taken one by one, then comes the wrist—or it may be called by him the trunk of a tree—from which the five branches, or fingers, spread out. What does the wrist of the hand stand for? It stands for Ahimsa, or absolute non-violence. This Ahimsa is the soul-force which binds all the social, economic and political programme together.

Such, then, is the extremely simple method of his village teaching, as he goes on his very long and infinitely arduous tours. At times I have accompanied him, and have watched his amazing moral determination to subdue his own body to his spirit's ardent call, in order to fulfil his mission. His frail bodily frame, racked by frequent illness, seems quite unable to bear the strain. But the miracle of soul-force, exercised by himself relentlessly in this manner, goes on repeating itself from day to day, without pause, until the end comes and he is imprisoned. The village people, whether Hindu or Musalman, will come from any distance to hear him. I have been with him in the Musalman areas of Bengal where the thronging crowd, eager to see him, and to follow his simple precepts, has been no less than among the Hindu villages. The "untouchables" are closest of all to his heart. He has adopted one of them as his own daughter, and has taken her, with willing consent, into orthodox Brahmin houses. Whenever, at a village gathering, the outcastes, or untouchables, are seated on the ground apart, he invariably goes and takes his seat among them. He then challenges the caste people to come near and join him, and they consent. Compared with other moral forces in India, his personality is the greatest. It makes no difference whether he visits the extreme North-West, or North-East, or the extreme South, the very same thing happens. The villagers flock to him as soon as ever they know that he is coming. I have been with him both in the South and in the North, as well as in the East and West, and it is easy for me to state this as a fact from what I have seen with my own eyes. My one anxiety has always been lest the crowd, which pressed forward to meet him and receive his blessing, should be so insistent in their devotion to him that injury might overtake him.

Just to show how far his name and influence are still penetrating among the countless millions of India, authentic records have been recently received of a whole tribe, untouched by civilization and living in a very remote and inaccessible part of the interior, which has given up its age-long habit of meat-eating and become vegetarian, solely because the news had reached the tribesmen that this was Gandhi's *hukm* (command). There are verifiable records concerning multitudes of aborigines who have determined to give up liquor in the same manner. To follow his precepts (and he will have no mere lip-service) may not mean any serious self-denial of daily comforts for the simple villagers; but it does mean the much harder sacrifice of those ingrained social prejudices which he continually condemns.

What has amazed me is to see young men and women, who, like the rich young man in the Gospel story, had great possessions, gladly changing their daily habits to a life of extreme hardship with the joy of a new-found freedom. Such is Jawaharlal Nehru, the son of Pandit Motilal Nehru, who was elected President of the National Congress for 1930, and is now in prison along with hundreds of others. Such was the young Muhammadan, Umar Sobhani, who died a short time ago, one of the richest young men in Bombay. Though he did not abandon his wealth, he was ready to suffer great hardship while following Mahatma Gandhi. Such, again, to-day is Shankarlal Banker—but the list would be far too long, if I tried to record it. Many of these had before, in earlier days, when they were young, adopted a Western mode of living, with all its comforts and luxuries. Then they met Mahatma Gandhi and were converted. Now they dress in *khaddar* and eat the simplest village food.

During this soul-force movement, which is still extending its area in unexpected ways, many thousands of persons, including women as well as men, have faced imprisonment and police violence as passive resisters, not only while Mahatma Gandhi was still at liberty, encouraging and inspiring them as their leader, but also with still greater fortitude and unity, if that were possible, since the time when he himself was imprisoned and they were left all alone. Eye-witnesses of these facts now include many Europeans, such as those whom the *Daily Telegraph* reported in Bombay as shocked by the violence exercised on passive resisters on what was called Black Saturday. There are also witnesses, such as Mr. K. Natarajan, the editor of the *Indian Social Reformer*, who made a visit to Dharasana in order to see what happened. The bare figures that have been given week by week in the House of Commons by the

Secretary of State, recording the number of political prisoners, are themselves an impressive witness. For it has always to be remembered that, for one person actually arrested and imprisoned, not seldom many hundreds of men and women have offered passive resistance. It would be hard, therefore, to find in the pages of modern history any close parallel to this moral influence of one single personality over vast bodies of people, or a more heroic record of sacrifice for a great cause. Garibaldi led his tattered regiments offering them imprisonment or death; but, heroic as that struggle was, it was a struggle of force against force, of violence against violence. In the Ruhr, men and women stood silently at bay till the French invasion broke; but violence was in their hearts, impotent as they were to use its weapons. Here men and women have gladly and joyfully stood up to serious bodily injury and rigorous imprisonment without any weapon in their hands and offering no resistance.[1]

These men and women who have thus gone joyfully to prison without offering any resistance have surely won the indefeasible right to speak for their fellow countrymen. Their own suffering and love have given them the power to interpret the inarticulate longings of those poor folk in India who cannot speak for themselves in the language of the West. This longing to have their own Government and to be governed by their own people is now wellnigh universal. The

[1] See Appendices II, IV and V.

villagers of India judge leadership by the one sovereign test of self-denial. Until the late C. R. Das in Bengal was prepared to sacrifice everything in the national cause, he did not gain from the common people the name of Deshbandhu.[1] Pandit Jawaharlal Nehru, as a rich young man, clothed in fine raiment, carried no weight at all. But Jawaharlal, clad in coarse home-spun, suffering joyfully in jail, fearless in the face of danger, becomes by universal choice the President of the National Congress and unchallenged leader of the Youth Movement.

The women of India are now taking upon themselves the same responsibility of suffering for the sake of their country. They uphold marvellously to-day the right of sacrifice for the cause, and as soon as ever they do so a throne is given to them in the hearts of the masses of the people. There is no greater change, and none more welcome, than this remarkable leadership of women in the one supreme endeavour to gain Indian independence. By this means alone more has been done in a few years to secure women's rights in India than by many generations of domestic submission. In this matter of the importance of woman in India the instinct of the Commissioners has guided them aright; and here in their recommendations they deserve full praise.

There is one scene in my memory concerning the flooded area of North Bengal, in 1922–23. It was one

[1] "Friend of the Country."

of those terrible disasters in which fifteen hundred square miles of cultivated land were flooded and the people were on the brink of starvation. The suffering was indescribable. The villages were Muhammadan, not Hindu; but every one of the national volunteers working with me was a Hindu, and nearly all the relief money came from Hindu sources. One hears frequently in London newspapers of Hindu-Muslim riots, but we hear nothing of a national movement in which religious differences are practically forgotten among the workers owing to the one great issue of the common cause. Day after day I went from one village to another with those national workers. Not once was the religious question ever broached between us. There has come a new, inclusive ideal of service, which preserves the devotion that was the religious strength of India in bygone days, but pours it out for the Motherland with a new religious meaning. This is itself bringing about an emancipation from all the narrow passions of the past. The nucleus of a national unity has been formed that is above race or party or creed. Even the old caste distinctions vanish, as this new devotion to India, the Motherland, gains ground. This has become a religious cult, and I have constantly seen the picture of India the Mother in students' rooms with the flowers of worship before it.

In Orissa the greatest misery of all exists among the poor who are attached to the soil. Floods come year after year and ruin husbandry. Late in the year

1927 eighty thousand houses were washed away. The Government, out of the famine relief fund and other sources, provided the pitiful sum of twelve shillings for the erection of each new house in which four or five persons were to be accommodated. Here again the national workers who came as volunteers and risked their lives in one of the most malignantly malarial parts of India differed widely in religion and social status. The help given reached us from distant parts as well as from near at hand. The clash came almost immediately between the Government subordinates and the nationalists who were out for Swaraj. The people were too sunk in misery to help themselves, but as soon as ever the national workers came their hopes revived. With the Government subordinate officers everything was done with an air of compulsion. People were ordered here and ordered there. The equipment required was extravagantly expensive compared with the methods of the volunteers. I tried my very hardest to work with both sides; but it was almost impossible. It was like mixing oil and water.

In the midst of these very difficulties word came that Mahatma Gandhi was about to arrive on one of his tours. Hope revived, and in a short time courage to deal with desperate human suffering returned. Then a sudden illness befell Mahatma Gandhi himself, and we feared a dangerous crisis because his blood pressure was very high. It was impossible, however, to prevent the poor half-starved people from flocking to see him, and getting what comfort they could from his presence. This one chance brought the only breath of spiritual exaltation they could ever have in their drab, monotonous lives. "Living skeletons" was the name that Gandhi gave to these poor people of Orissa, and the title was terribly true.

A little later on, after Mahatma Gandhi had passed on to the National Congress at Madras, nearly a thousand downtrodden peasants came in from a neighbouring State with stories of harsh oppression. The Rajah, they said, had wasted his substance in luxury, not having to render any account for the taxes he levied from his own subjects. At last the misery had gone beyond all bounds, and great numbers had left the State in order to ask for justice. Month after month they waited, with a patience like that of Job, refusing to go back till their sufferings were remedied. Here again it was a band of national workers who kept these poor people from utter starvation. While we hear in England about the treaty rights of the princes, which must be strictly observed, we hear little of the rights of these poor people from whom the puppet Rajah derives his revenue with the help of the military power of Great Britain. These starving peasants turned to us to deliver them from their misery.

All along, if I have made my point clear, this new

national life is stirring, and the people are responding. At Chandpur, in the cholera camp, the clash came in a different way between the national workers and the officials. The Government had sent down an array of sub-assistant surgeons and compounders of medicine with their regulation equipment, under an officer from the Indian Medical Service; but the poor people who were suffering would have none of them. They openly preferred the help of the national volunteers, who had come first to their aid in their distress. With incredible speed a makeshift for a hospital had been arranged with different sheds. Volunteers offered themselves up to three times the number we required. A doctor, dressed in homespun, wearing a Gandhi cap, was in command. The work was brilliantly carried through, and the epidemic was stayed. But one could see in the midst of it all how the poorest of the poor clung closely to the national workers. One of the latter sacrificed his own life in the service of the poor, and others were very seriously ill. Some returned with health shattered. Musalman volunteers were helping side by side with Hindu compatriots. Meanwhile the Government medical officer and his staff were stranded. They had no patients. By the greatest effort of conciliation I was able to get the Government officials taken into the national work for a few days. But the scheme broke down, as I feared from the start. Their methods were entirely different. But the experiment proved how cumbrous and expensive the Government scheme was, and I saw at the same time how remarkably cheap and efficient the National Congress organization had become. Among those to be cared for and nursed back to health at Chandpur were those who came from the untouchable classes. But the volunteers made no caste or religious distinctions. Since that time I have followed the history of this national doctor who managed the whole of this organization so efficiently and cheaply. He has been in jail again and again, and is even now suffering imprisonment as a passive resister.

An amusing story may light up some of the darkness of the picture I have been drawing. The Bishop in Assam, the Right Rev. Pakenham Walsh, together with his wife, who was a skilled hospital nurse, suddenly appeared in the camp one day and asked to be taken on. We had only just recovered from the final split with the Government officials, and it was very difficult for me to explain the fine point of distinction that the Bishop in Assam was not under Government control. Indeed, I never tried to do so, but explained instead unblushingly that he and his wife were both Irish Free Staters. That made an impression; yet still there was some suspicion, for though the Bishop did not wear gaiters, nevertheless his clothes were not made of the orthodox *khaddar* which nationalists wear. However, we got over that difficulty by my telling the volunteers that they were dear friends of mine, and asking that a trial should be given them. With a thoroughness that did the volunteers credit they at once set the Bishop to carry the cholera buckets to the latrine, and he did it with such zest that he was soon admitted as a volunteer worker. When I returned to the camp (after a discreet absence while he was making his own footing) I found him diligently carrying the slops, and his wife nursing a tiny, wee orphan baby of three weeks old whose father and mother had both died of cholera only the day before.

One thing I would wish to make as clear as possible. In this national upheaval which I have described religious differences between Hindus and Musalmans become obliterated. The creed of nationalism is by far the greatest levelling factor in modern India. It makes for unification.

CHAPTER IV

THE NATIONAL PROGRAMME

The reason for the continuance of the non-co-operation movement repeated again and again by Mahatma Gandhi is this—that Swaraj, or self-government, has become now an absolute necessity, if national reforms are to go forward. India can look after her own affairs much better than Great Britain can, because the British rule is foreign, and therefore extravagant; official, instead of human; and through lack of understanding very often oppressive.[1]

He believes it is also directed on all crucial occasions more to the good of England than to the welfare of India. Again and again he has put forward a simple test—whether, for instance, the British Government is ready to remit the salt tax, which oppresses the very poorest of the poor; or to abolish the sale of cheap Government opium to mothers who dope their babies; or to encourage home-spinning among the peasants in the numberless villages of India, and thus save them from relying solely upon agriculture and leading a half-starved existence; or to prohibit the sale of thoroughly bad "country" liquor in the villages, from which Government revenue is derived; or to reduce the extravagant expenditure on New Delhi; or, again, on foreign troops from Great Britain at five

[1] See Appendices I–IV.

times the expense (for each man) of an Indian soldier. But the Government remains silent.

As one who has lived among the villagers, to me personally these seem to be matters that ought to be reasoned over. They should have been brought to a conference long ago. Questions of this kind ought surely to be thrashed out, and what is really good for India should be decided.

Yet there is one thing, perhaps, more than anything else that stands in the way of such a process. The central power in India is not a responsible Government. It can flout public opinion whenever it cares to do so. What this means in practice we can hardly grasp in Great Britain, where the Government is responsible to public opinion not merely through a vote in Parliament, but through an authoritative Press.

Along with power in India goes prestige. No Government that ever existed has given up power, already within its own control, without a struggle; and the Indian Government is no exception. When the present Prime Minister was in India more than twenty years ago he told me with a laugh what he had said at Simla, when he met the Viceroy's Executive Council. The phrase was so apt that it has stuck in my mind ever since. "Gentlemen," he said, "a Government of Archangels couldn't help going wrong and making dreadful mistakes without an Opposition. Where is your Leader of the Opposition?"

To my own way of thinking, Mahatma Gandhi has been the most effective "Leader of the Opposition" that the Government of India has ever had. For the first time in recent history the highest authorities at Simla have had someone to stand up to them. For instance, he put forward in 1921 his remarkable proposition that if only the Government of India would actively promote home-spinning and weaving in the villages and actively prohibit the sale of intoxicating liquor and drugs, he would find in this a basis for co-operation. At that critical moment I took this proposal personally to the Government, and made it as clear as possible that Mahatma Gandhi meant exactly what he said. But there was absolutely no response.

If the reason be asked it will be found in the one fact that all the power was in their hands and not in the hands of Mahatma Gandhi. Therefore imperial prestige would not allow anything that might be regarded as weakness. The Government of India, so the official argument would run, knew much better what was good for the people of India than did Mr. Gandhi; at any rate, they were not going to be dictated to under threats of non-co-operation. Let him call off his non-co-operation first, and then the Government of India would be ready to reason about it afterwards. This is always the argument of a Government entrenched behind the barrier of irresponsible power.

Two instances may suffice of the harm that is done

by the exercise of such arbitrary rule. In 1919 the Rowlatt Act was introduced, whereby a man might be imprisoned without any open trial on evidence given by the police. To anyone who knows the corrupt state of the whole police system in India this Rowlatt Act opened the door to evils of the worst possible character. The Right Hon. V. Srinavasa Sastri, in a prophetic speech, warned the Government of India of the consequences of forcing through such a measure. But the Government owed no responsibility to Indian public opinion, however enlightened and united. All the subsequent troubles, including "Amritsar" itself, followed from this high-handed action of an irresponsible Government. For it led at once to civil disobedience.

A second instance may be found in the doubling of the Salt Tax in the year 1923. During the post-war years Indian finances were suffering as a result of fluctuations in currency, and it was regarded as necessary to show a surplus budget. The Government of India proposed, therefore, that the Salt Tax itself should be doubled in order to balance the accounts. But even the hardiest Government supporter among the elected members could not bear that! For the evil of the Salt Tax is this, that it inflicts injury upon the millions of the very poorest people who are living on the verge of starvation. To double the Salt Tax was to create for these poorest people a double hardship at a time when the cost of living was terribly high already. So a vote was taken in the Assembly and the Government proposal was defeated. But that adverse vote in the Assembly did not end the matter. On the contrary, the Viceroy at once certificated the doubling of the Salt Tax against the will of the elected members. Yet by the end of the financial year it was proved beyond a shadow of doubt that there had been no need to double this tax at all; for there was an ample surplus. Therefore the Salt Tax went back to its old level after the year's futile experiment was over.

The power in the Viceroy's hands was absolute. He had only to sign a piece of paper and the vote of the Assembly was cancelled. Truly Mr. Ramsay Macdonald, if he came out to India again, might still repeat to the Executive Council at Simla his word of wisdom: "Gentlemen," he would say, "a Government of Archangels couldn't help going wrong and making dreadful mistakes without an Opposition. Where is your Leader of the Opposition?"

But Mahatma Gandhi, the "Leader of the Opposition", is in prison, and the Simon Report recommends that the Central Government of India should remain in future, for all practical purposes, as irresponsible as ever.

The question may be asked with some impatience: "What is your alternative? Would not things immediately break down if the British left? Are we not in India as trustees for the poorest people in order to prevent their being exploited by the rich? Have we not a trustee's duty to hand over the Government to responsible persons instead of letting everything go to rack and ruin?"

At this point let me make clear, by an obvious analogy, that it is psychologically impossible to keep India in leading-strings any longer. In these modern times, with their modern methods of government, India has obviously reached what may be called her political age of discretion. In the home life of any family there comes that awkward age when to exercise restraint any longer only aggravates the trouble and drives the spirit of revolt still deeper. We all recognize that such a revolt is healthy, and that the time comes when there must be absolute freedom of inner choice and self-direction if growth is not to be stunted. Such a time has come in India, and it is already long overdue. In the different chapters which follow I shall show into what a vicious circle India had come owing to the prolonged subjection to foreign rule which had enmeshed her and crippled her freedom. It will also be made clear how it was the advent of the volcanic personality of Mahatma Gandhi which broke through that vicious circle. All this will be argued out later; but at this point it needs to be made clear that for the present regime to go on longer unchanged at the centre, as the Simon Commissioners suggest, is now not only psychologically but also politically impossible. It is leading to an ever-increasing estrangement, and also to the final imposition of a foreign political structure which has faulty cracks in it already, and is becoming more and more unsuited to the genius of the country.

One thing may be regarded as certain. The national programme of India will be a very different thing from that which the Simon Commissioners now contemplate. There will be no mere patching up of an old garment with new bits of cloth here and there, such as will make the rent worse. There will be no putting new wine into old bottles. Thus, for instance, the army will never be left outside the body of Indian national life under British control. There will also be no more a bureaucratic Government at Simla, irresponsible to Indian opinion and under the dictation of the India Office at Whitehall. Nor will there be a Secretary of State for India, with his Council, looking down from his official building upon Clive's statue, as the emblem of British occupation. It is very doubtful indeed whether the analogy of "dominion status" will hold for long, since India can never by any stretch of imagination be in perpetuity a "Dominion" like Canada or Australia. An entirely different terminology will be needed for the bond of connection between India and Great Britain. If, as Sir Henry Lawrence contemplated, an alliance on terms of equal friendship can be brought about by future statesmanship, that will represent a link of interdependence which may benefit both peoples. It is in that direction of alliance rather than in the direction of a dominion that the British connection with India may lie in the future.

The new life in India will cut its own channels; but more and more it will be found that the peculiar genius of the people lies in the villages. There first of all Mahatma Gandhi's programme will be put into active operation. For India is a country of villages. Taken as village units, the five hundred thousand villages of British India should not prove an insurmountable number to deal with. Each village will have its own individual development as a self-contained unit, and its own living bonds of connection with its next-door neighbours. This system of village "republics", each with its own President and *panchayat*,[1] carrying on its own Swaraj, is likely to be the national objective. From this fundamental village system, if Mahatma Gandhi is right, the new body politic of India, when the British occupation is over, will come into being. It will have the character of ancient India about it, and it will appeal to the peculiar instinct of those who have inhabited the Indian peninsula from time immemorial. No dynasty or empire, either of the Moghuls or of the British, has been able to destroy it, though each invader who has come as a foreigner from outside has done something to shake it. For Mahatma Gandhi, as he looks out upon the Indian future, the village *is* India in miniature. India, to him, represents the rural as contrasted

[1] Village committee of five members.

with the urban civilization. The genius of the one differs from the genius of the other. The world can contain both, when Indians are allowed to govern themselves without interference from a different type of civilization. Bombay and Calcutta are rather excrescences on the true body politic of India than normal, natural growths. They will regain their proper dimensions as the village life recovers itself. They will no longer suck away, at the extremities of the body, the life-blood which ought to nourish and support the village nerve-centres.

Once more, the different provincial areas of India will obviously not remain in the confusion that is still too much in evidence. To-day, language areas which are obviously homogeneous are cut across in a manner that has sacrificed the genius of the people themselves to mere administrative convenience. The national Congress leaders, under the inspiration of Mahatma Gandhi, have already begun to remedy, in their own Congress affairs, the impossible conditions existing in British India. Let me take one instance which is very familiar to me. The Uriya-speaking people of Orissa have been linked, for purely administrative purposes, with the Hindi-speaking province of Behar. Other Uriyas are to be found in the northern section of Madras. The whole language area is broken up. At one time Orissa was linked on to Bengal. Thus these Uriyas have been thrown about from one province to another in hopeless confusion. Yet nowhere in the whole of India was there more need to appeal to regional patriotism in order to raise the Uriya villagers themselves from a poverty which has become more and more desperate. The National Congress has encouraged a much more rational division. It has taken the same course with regard to the different language areas in the Madras Presidency and also in Bombay.

Here, in the last instance I have mentioned, the Simon Report has made, on the whole, very sound suggestions. With regard also to the separation of Burma from India there seem to me good reasons advanced. In matters of administrative efficiency of this kind there are very many improvements of a valuable character suggested in the Report. I should personally regard, for example, the responsibility for law and order now to be handed over to the provincial Governments as an important step in the right direction, if the responsibility is made complete and not surrounded by safeguards. On the other hand, to do this in the provinces while leaving the central Government practically unchanged is surely a wrong course to follow. That at least is my tentative judgment.

On these and other matters, however, my own personal opinion should obviously not be pressed; for I have made it quite clear in my preface that technical administration matters of this kind, however important, are beyond the scope of what I have set out to explain. If, therefore, I am asked to map out in detail where I agree and where I disagree with the Report, I should answer that my main purpose does not lie in that direction. For I am an Englishman, and it cannot be repeated too often that the very meaning of self-government is that these things shall be settled by Indians themselves and not by Englishmen at all. The mistake from first to last has been the refusal to allow to Indians the initiative in these matters so that they might follow out to the end their own national ideals.

They will undoubtedly make many mistakes. But the mistakes will be their own, and the blame for them will be their own. They will not be able any longer to lay them upon others and thus weaken themselves.

In Great Britain, also, in spite of our favoured insular position, we had to proceed by the same method of making mistakes, however costly. We made them ourselves by the score. We had rebellions and revolutions. But all the while we were learning self-government. It is surely reasonable to expect that Indian national leaders will act in the same manner. The less adventurous souls may wish to remain still longer under the old shelter of British protection. The more adventurous spirits will seek to go forth into the unknown without a moment's delay.

If it be argued that only destructive criticism is being offered in India and that constructive effort is needed, then surely I have made it plain from what I have already stated about Mahatma Gandhi's programme and the National Congress's acceptance of it, that such a general charge is unfair. Already in many ways, as I have seen with my own eyes in the villages, the National Congress workers have taken the lead in constructive work—not always, it is true, wisely and well, but with an enthusiasm and self-sacrifice that have constantly put others to shame.

For instance, in forwarding everywhere Mahatma Gandhi's village industrial *khaddar* scheme Congress workers have been performing a national economic service. I have seen the results in a steady growth of prosperity in those villages where the whole programme has been actively adopted. In order to help the villagers national volunteers, both men and women, have gone down to live and work in the villages among the poor people as their friends. The whole social programme of Mahatma Gandhi is being carried forward by these Congress workers. In consequence, untouchability is being given up, drink and drugs have been less used, the evils of child marriage have been lessened, and other important reforms have been carried through. Above all, it is noticeable that women have joined in the National Movement in ever-increasing numbers. The Simon Report has taken admirable notice of the importance of woman's share in the political sphere, and one of the best recommendations in the whole two volumes is that which encourages in every way the entrance of women into the political life of the country. Here is a point where the National Congress has already gone forward in the most active manner. For it is essentially a democratic body, and it has steadily set its face against any compromise on the question of class, creed, or sex. Women have exactly the same rights as men. Women have already been elected Presidents of the National Congress itself and on its executive committee.

Thus, from what we see happening before our eyes under the impulse for social and economic reform which Mahatma Gandhi has given by his personal inspiration and enthusiasm, every part of the political organism will be transformed by Indian national leaders themselves from the present essentially foreign British rule into something more indigenous. The Indian people must choose their own leaders and follow them and correct them when they go astray. There is no other course that leads to freedom. But this is not possible until self-government, delegated from the people and responsible to the people, is handed over to Indian representatives not only in the provinces, but at the centre.

CHAPTER V

A CHANGED MENTAL OUTLOOK

It has been necessary to give at some length, through different illustrations, a picture of the times we are painfully passing through in India, times comparable only to some great religious and social revolution touching every side of human life and renewing the face of the earth. For it is just in relation to all this that the Commissioners who have given us the Simon Report have suffered a very grievous loss owing to the unfortunate conditions under which they went out. If only it had been possible for them, under the right guidance, to have travelled as private persons, meeting Mahatma Gandhi himself in an entirely informal manner in his own Ashram and sharing the atmosphere in which his followers spend their lives, then their ideas about the future constitution of India would have been profoundly modified. For they would have seen all those inner social forces at work which escape the notice of the ordinary traveller and of the government official also.

At the height of the non-co-operation movement a wave of social reform swept over Bengal. I was present at a gathering in the country where the chief landlord of the district, a stout elderly man, had been called upon to take the chair. The other landlords were seated on each side of him in a semicircle and the poor people had gathered in vast numbers. The students sang stirring patriotic songs and everyone was deeply moved. The speaker, who had come down from the National Congress, called on the poor people to give up their bad habits of taking liquor and opium. At the close of his fervent address he called forward a ragged old man, who was evidently an opium-eater, to come forward and take the pledge. The shrunken, ragged man stood trembling before the audience and then raised his voice and said, pointing towards the Chairman: "Yes, I will take the pledge if he also will take a pledge with me." The Chairman asked nervously in reply: "What pledge do you want me to take?" "Promise", said the man in rags, "that you will no longer oppress the poor!" The audience, who knew the old landlord's evil reputation for usury, took up the cry. "Yes," said they, "take the pledge with him!" Then the Chairman stood up before the meeting and acknowledged the wrong he had done, and the two old men took their mutual pledges together.

It is the sight of incidents such as these, which are continually occurring in varied forms under the new national impulse, that I could have desired the Commissioners to experience. For things like these leave behind them an ineffaceable impression of reality. They reveal what Mahatma Gandhi has called the inner Swaraj already won. They show human life taking new social forms. Knowing, therefore, from direct practical experience the great gulf fixed between the official world, with its huge secretariats and offices, and this real, concrete world of humanity in which my everyday life in India is passed, it is natural that I should miss from the Report the keen air of reform from within, which I have been breathing in India, especially in recent years, since Mahatma Gandhi captured the minds and hearts of the people. The miracle of change has been his own creation.

Bearing this in mind, I cannot but feel that the Commissioners' lack of insight into the Gandhi Movement and all it denotes represents such a serious failure in the Report that it must carry untoward consequences with it. It is true that Mahatma Gandhi is referred to, but it is usually with a shade of annoyance, as though he were wholly an obstructionist, and a dangerous rebel. His paramount importance as a constructive leader is not recognized at all. There is hardly a sign of clear, intimate knowledge of the positive changes he had made throughout the whole fabric of Indian society, literally revolutionizing, as no one has ever done for centuries past, the mentality of the Indian village people, taking away from them all sense of fear of those who have hitherto ruled over them, so that the old submission and subservience have departed.[1]

Once an Indian friend, who differed from me in politics, condemned in my presence the whole non-

[1] See Appendix VI

co-operation movement, wherein I had taken an active and sympathetic part.

"If only", he exclaimed bitterly, "we had spent our energies in working the Reform Constitution, which had been given us as a gift by Great Britain, instead of wasting our time in futile non-co-operation, we should have got at least a hundred per cent. further forward to-day than we are at present."

He then began blaming Gandhi for this futility, as he called it. When he had ended his tirade I put to him a simple question.

"Does the Indian villager to-day", I asked, "stand up to the Englishman more fearlessly than before? Has he become less afraid of the Government official, of the landowner, and of the police?"

My friend paused suddenly, as if a new thought had struck him for the first time.

"You're right," he said, "I never thought of that! Of course, there's no comparison! The villager looks every man in the face to-day."

What has really come to pass in India has been that which I have called a changed mentality. There has been attained, over large areas of the country, a new, fearless outlook that is nothing less than revolutionary. The consequences of this have been very far-reaching indeed. In many important respects, owing to this new movement, the Simon Report has become already out of date. For it has lost touch with the exceedingly rapid current of recent events. Nothing in the whole of its two large volumes caused me such a shock of surprise as the following passage, which the Commissioners have unanimously signed:—

> "In writing this Report", they say, "we have made no allusion to the events of the last few months in India. In fact, the whole of our principal recommendations were arrived at and unanimously agreed upon before these events occurred. We have not altered a line of our Report on that account; for it is necessary to look beyond particular incidents and to take a longer view."

If the events referred to in this passage were merely ephemeral, if they represented only an effervescence rising up like a bubble on the surface of Indian Society, to die down again the next moment and disappear, then such placid lack of interest on the part of the Commissioners might have some justification behind it. But if, as appears to me quite certain, the whole structure of Indian Society is being refashioned under the stress of an impelling power from within, then to ignore altogether this new force, with its strong creative impulse, as though it were of no practical importance, is an attitude that can only lead in the end to very grievous misunderstanding.

The Simon Report is in its true element when it deals with statistical details concerning the administration, suggesting here and there the necessary changes for the smoother working of the present cumbrous machine, but it has not mastered the inner problems of the new national life of modern India, which is making breaches in the old political channels in every direction. It has as its objective, not the rapidly changing India, which will be still more vividly active in the near future, overpassing and sweeping away the landmarks of the past, but rather that stratified and stationary India which the officials have carefully tabulated and dealt with from time immemorial, treating it as if it would always remain the same. For, like the dullest of the French encyclopædists on the eve of the French Revolution, the different secretariats of the Government of India continue to pour out their volumes of statistics, while the vast upheaval of human life from the lowest strata of society escapes their attention.

Yet all the while, active, vital, emotional, throbbing with new energy, the National Movement is there, not only in India, but in every country of Asia, and it is very rapidly spreading over every part of Africa also. This is the one mighty revolutionary force pervading the Eastern world to-day. "India and the World's Peace" is the title of Norman Angell's July number of *Foreign Affairs*. In this single issue we are shown that the repercussions of the Indian revolution are manifest in Palestine and Syria; in Indo-China and the Far East; in Cyrenaica, Tunis, and Egypt.

To ignore so completely these revolutionary days

might have been put down as an act of obscurantism; but the truth appears rather to have been that their minds were so overwhelmed with the mass of official material presented to them, their journeys were so scheduled for them according to tabulated routine, that they missed these interior forces in their main reckoning. That such a thing is quite possible I can vouch for personally by an incident that happened in my own experience in India with regard to a certain Deputy Commissioner in Delhi who shall remain anonymous. I came to him to ask him to take some interest in the National Movement, which was almost violently active outside his very door. In my eagerness, I offered to put him into close touch with it. He turned to me, with a weary look, from his desk: "Just look at those files", he said to me. That was all, but it spoke volumes. There were files of utterly useless petitions and counter-petitions which Sir John Simon and his Commissioners had wearily to wade through, and the same effect has been produced that was noticeable in my friend at Delhi.

It was fully to be expected that a Report, dealing with the external matters of India only slightly known in the West, would at once command public attention and receive commendation in Great Britain. It has given the British people valuable information about many things which they very much wanted to know. It has also been written from the British point of view and is, therefore, easily intelligible for British readers.

But in the long run it represents what is in reality a British solution of the Indian question, and it is impossible not to observe how, from the very first, even guardedly moderate Indian opinion has expressed its disapproval of the main conclusions reached. To Indians themselves the spectacular part of the first volume, called the Survey, was only a distraction. They did not need to go over all that material again. To them, the controversial issues came in the second volume. And it has been just at this point that the solutions proposed by the Commissioners have come under condemnation. The British newspapers have already discounted this condemnation as implying a hasty judgment. But this is not true. For the opposition is led by such sober thinkers as the Right Hon. V. Srinavasa Sastri of Madras, Sir Tej Bahadur Sapru of Allahabad, and Sir Chimanlal Setalvad of Bombay —to mention three leading names only. The carefully considered verdict of three Indian statesmen such as these cannot easily be brushed aside as immaterial. Even the progressive Muhammadans appear to be dissatisfied by the reactionary character of the Report, and claim that the reforms should go much further.

In spite of all this pronounced opposition, the expectation is still being continually held out in Great Britain that, after the first stormy outburst in India has passed over, most people will settle down and seek to be satisfied with the advantages that the Report offers. It is hoped that, as a thunderstorm which first breaks in a deluge of rain then clears the air, so a clearer political atmosphere will arise in India after the first thunderous storm has blown over.

But such a hopeful forecast of the future is obviously at fault. These men who have criticized the Report are eminent Indians, and India is their own country. They have had their home-life in India, and their whole tradition has been intimately bound up with their own people. For long years they have pondered day and night over those very problems upon which the Commissioners have spent only two years. If now these opinions of the Simon Commissioners are imposed upon the people of India from without, against their own consent, this is likely to be only another instance of that purely British interference in Indian affairs which Indians more and more resent.

Meanwhile the inner movement among the people is gathering strength from each fresh act of repression, as such movements have always done in every age. It is attracting like a magnet all the vitally progressive forces that lie within the field of its operation. The events that are taking place in India, the indomitable courage of the passive resisters, the bravery of the women, the heroism of the Sikhs—all these events have struck the imagination of youth and great things are being accomplished. Common suffering and deepened sympathy are welding the people together. A changed mental outlook has come which carries us far beyond the recommendations of the Simon Report.

CHAPTER VI

THE SHAME OF SUBJECTION

I have dwelt at some length in my opening chapter upon the hardship and suffering that are being experienced both in India and Great Britain to-day as an after-effect of the European War; and I have pointed out how in the everyday life continually led in India among the poor this picture of human suffering has always been prominently before me. But it would be entirely wrong to treat all this as though it were an unmixed evil. On the contrary it represents to me one of the most hopeful means whereby India and Great Britain may in the end come to understand one another. For it brings with it, in Great Britain especially, a growing capacity to look the hard facts of life in the face without flinching. It disturbs our phlegmatic British equanimity and forces us to think intelligently. It drives us away from the comfortable, conventional view that everything would go well with us if only people did not make a fuss. Thus it sends us back to our own inner resources. All this is to the good, for it tends to make us humble.

There is one other good in it all which is of no slight practical importance. In the heyday of imperial power, Great Britain had become so profoundly convinced of her own mission as the world's benefactor, while making handsome profits all the while, that the Pharisaic spirit had crept in which kept saying, "Lord, I thank Thee that I am not as other men are." The hypocrisy of all this had become intolerable for the rest of the world. But the realization at last that others have become far more efficient than ourselves has humbled us. The imperialist mentality is by no means in the ascendant to-day in Great Britain as it was earlier in the century.

One positive result has been reached. The Simon Commission Report has created a very deep interest about India that had never existed before. There has arisen throughout Great Britain an earnest desire to learn. Thus, through mutual suffering has come experience and humility; and these two things are equally necessary for a right understanding. Now, to-day, India and Great Britain are standing opposite each other with a far greater sense of reality and a much deeper seriousness of purpose. It is felt on all sides that we need the truth, the whole truth, and nothing but the truth. For, whatever happens, everyone is agreed that the present strained situation cannot go on indefinitely. Therefore, in what follows, I shall attempt to deal mainly with the larger issues which must frankly be faced by each one of us if we would judge aright the immediate constitutional problem with which the Simon Commission deals.

Why, then, are Indians feeling intensely to-day, as they have never felt so acutely before, that though other important and highly necessary things may be put on one side, this struggle with Great Britain to obtain their own independence cannot possibly be postponed any longer? What is this insistent urge from within which has come into such prominence, as the one driving force behind the National Movement—so strong and insistent that it has drawn thousands of men and women, young and old alike, fearlessly to face untold hardships without striking a blow, and to offer themselves for rigorous imprisonment which may end in the ruin of themselves and their families?

There are different answers which might be given to these questions, but here I shall give one historical explanation which has strongly appealed to me for many years past; for it appears to me to go down to the root of the whole matter and to show the ultimate reason for the present political unrest. Much of what I shall give to Western readers for the first time in this book has already been thoroughly discussed in India through pamphlets and articles which I have published. It has, therefore, already been put to the test in India, and has passed through a critical examination over there. It may be taken as representing a general Indian point of view.

Fifty years ago there was an important book written by Sir John Seeley concerning the relation at that time between India and Great Britain. It was called *The Expansion of England.* Seeley wrote it during a very pronounced imperialistic period in Great Britain's colonial history. It was that critical epoch when Africa was being divided up among the Western Powers—Germany, Great Britain, France, Italy, Portugal, Belgium, were all staking out their claims as if the whole earth was to be divided up between them. Seeley's famous book bears all the marks of that "expansion" period, and its very title tells the same story. India is looked upon not so much as a distinct and separate entity in herself, but rather as forming a major part of England's vast world expansion. Little is said about any benefit that has accrued to India, though that is taken for granted. But the thesis, which is all-important to the historian, is the method whereby the small, grey-clouded, northern island of Great Britain by some providential good fortune came into possession of a whole continent in the South of Asia called India, and occupied it at a most critical time, when the colonies in North America had been lost. The failure on one side of the world was compensated by this unexpected success in the East. The American losses were made up to Great Britain by the Indian gains.

Before discussing this conception of the inter-relationship between Great Britain and India it is well to pause for a moment and think seriously what the thesis itself implies and how humiliating to India it is. It represents a pre-war attitude that is almost inconceivable among students of history to-day. Whatever remains beneath the surface, as an inheritance of the race, Great Britain can hardly be so outspokenly self-confident and self-centred in her imperial ambitions as she was in Seeley's time, fifty years ago. For now it may truly be said that among thoughtful people all over the world the very word "Empire" has begun to have a sinister connotation and to demand an apology for using it.

Seeley is quite frank in the picture which he draws of the early "expansion" of Great Britain in the East. He has no illusions about its actual character and conduct; and as history comes to be rewritten in a scientific manner and the truth told by incontestable documentary facts, the eighteenth century in India presents a very sordid picture on the British side. We came as freebooters, eager to make money quickly. We gambled with death in a horrible tropical climate. Some made their fortune and got away with it back to England; thousands died of typhoid or malaria, or through debauchery or drink. It was in no sense the sober, moral element of England that went out to the East. There was no possible basis of comparison between this Eastern exodus and that of the Pilgrim Fathers to the West. The two streams of colonization were poles apart. Seeley rightly points out that these British "nabobs" (as they were called) brought degradation to England on their return as well as to India during their short stay. There was a phrase invented—"shaking the pagoda tree"—which has passed into the English language. It reveals the whole sordid process. The amount of wealth that was ruthlessly looted from India by these freebooting agents of a wealthy trading company is difficult to estimate. But it must have been indescribably great, and it sowed the seeds of poverty, degradation, and ignorance by overturning the whole economic fabric of society. I have already quoted in a book called *Christ and Labour* the documentary evidence for this from the East India Company's own records; how, after the most terrible recorded famine in Indian history, when one out of three of the population had perished from starvation, Warren Hastings, the Governor, congratulates the Company on having been able forcibly to keep up the revenue, and even to increase it.

In a book quite recently written by Lieutenant-Colonel Arthur Osburn, D.S.O., under the title *Must England Lose India?* [1] a picture is given of this period, similar to Sir John Seeley's. From it I quote the following:—

> "We raided and plundered, settled and intrigued on the rich coasts of India, much as our Danish ancestors had raided the 'Saxon shores' and the coast of East Anglia. Vast fortunes were brought back to England from India by unknown adventurers, some of whom had been scarcely ten years absent—and few questions were asked. So we

[1] Published by Alfred A. Knopf, London and New York. MCMXXX.

> sucked India dry, until English observers compared India to a 'squeezed lemon'. Accounts written by Englishmen, after the first hundred years of English rule and English interference, make ghastly reading."

The small book by Sir John Seeley is a blunt, outspoken volume, and it bears out the picture of the eighteenth century given by Lieutenant-Colonel Osburn. Many of the things that are said in Seeley's *Expansion* are neither flattering to India nor creditable to Great Britain. But they deserve to be closely studied nevertheless; for they bring us to the heart of the whole problem. Here is one of the main points of his argument:—

> "If ever", he says, "there would arise in India a nationality movement similar to that which we have witnessed in Italy, the English power could not even make the resistance that was made in Italy by Austria but must succumb at once. For what means can England have, which is not a military state, of resisting the rebellion of two hundred and fifty millions of subjects?
>
> "Do you say, as we conquered them before, we could conquer them again? But I explained that we did not conquer them. I showed you that out of the army which won our victories, four-fifths consisted of native troops. That we were able to

> hire these native troops for service in India was due to the fact that the feeling of nationality had no existence there."

So far as this passage is concerned, Sir John Seeley merely emphasizes the one point, which has often been referred to since, that England did not conquer India, but only holds dominion there on account of the people's own acquiescence in her rule. It is all the more necessary, therefore, to mark carefully the sentences which follow. Sir John Seeley continues:

> "Now if the feeling of a common nationality began to exist there only feebly; if, without inspiring any active desire to drive out the foreigner, it only created a notion that it was shameful to assist him in maintaining his dominion—from that day, almost, our Empire would cease to exist. It is a condition of our Indian Empire that it should be held without any great effort. As it was acquired without much effort on the part of the English state, it must be retained in the same way. We are not prepared to bury millions and millions, or army upon army, in defending our acquisition. The moment India began to show herself what we so idly imagine her to be, a conquered nation, that moment we should recognize perforce the impossibility of retaining her."

A very small movement often shows which way the wind is blowing. It is easy to mark the current of Indian opinion to-day by pointing out what words in this passage of Seeley's book have already become offensive. The word "native", for instance, is bitterly resented, when it is used by British residents as the common name for Indians themselves. There is no surer way for an Englishman in India to reveal his own mentality than this use of the word "native" instead of the word "Indian". So pronounced has this sentiment become in the last twenty years that the Government of India has forbidden the use of the term "native" in official documents.

It may be of some value at this point to tell a story about Lord Morley with regard to such an offence. He was making a speech in the House of Commons wherein he desired to be specially friendly and conciliatory. It was an appeal for good will. But no one in the India Office had corrected his terminology, and he continually spoke of Indians as "natives". The moment that I read the full report of the speech, as it was cabled out to India, this one word jarred; and I was certain that it would give great offence. When I went over to the common room of the College, where our professors used to forgather before lectures, I came into the very thing I had feared. Our staff was almost entirely Indian and they were very kindly and friendly people. But as one of them, standing up in the midst of the circle of listeners, read to his audience the reported speech, he laid the very slightest emphasis on the word "natives" each time it occurred; and I could see the listeners almost wince at each repetition. Half the conciliatory effect of Lord Morley's speech had been lost even on that cultured and friendly audience by this unconscious breach of good manners on Lord Morley's part. And yet it was Lord Morley himself who gave us, if I remember aright, the admirable dictum that bad manners in India were worse than a blunder; they were a crime. A few years later, Mr. Charles Roberts, whose sensitive desire to respect Indian feeling had become almost a passion, referred to this story, which I had told in an earlier volume: He was greatly disturbed: "How is it possible", he said to me, "for us at this distance to avoid such an offence against good manners, when English men and women who have come over from India habitually use this word 'native' about the Indians in our presence?" I could only answer him that this was part of the tragedy of trying to rule a vast country like India at seven thousand miles' distance. Yet when national feeling is rising it is at these delicately sensitive points that the greatest injury is caused by the use of a clumsy word. "Our Empire in India" would give equal offence to-day. The revolt against any form of subjection has now sprung up from within. Every time that Mahatma Gandhi has gone through the villages, passing on from one province to another, he has stirred up wherever he has gone just that "feeling of a common nationality" which Sir John Seeley had claimed to be non-existent in India in his own day. We have seen, on every side, what Seeley calls "the notion created that it was shameful to assist the foreigner in maintaining his dominion".

CHAPTER VII

THE VICIOUS CIRCLE ENTERED

In seeking to represent the atmosphere of modern India, with all its ardent hopes, longings and aspirations, I have to go forward step by step with an argument whose purport will become clear as I go on. I must ask the British reader's patience, because the whole meaning of the word "subjection" is foreign to him and he has never experienced its bad results. He little realizes how hard it is to escape from the vicious circle it creates when once this circle has been entered.

There is a further passage in Seeley's book which gives as early as the year 1882 an abstract discussion of the subject of independence that now has become a matter of life and death to modern India.

"If India", he says, "does at last begin to breathe as a single national whole—and our own rule is perhaps doing more than ever was done by former Governments to make this possible—then there would be needed no explosion of despair. . . . The moment that a mutiny is threatened, which shall be no mere mutiny, but the expression of a universal feeling of nationality, at that same moment all hope is at an end —as all desire ought to be at an end—of preserving our Empire. For we are not really conquerors of India and we cannot rule India as conquerors; if we undertake to do so, it is not necessary to inquire whether we could succeed; for we should assuredly be ruined financially by the mere attempt."

One thing appears to me to come out with conspicuous clearness. Indian independence is primarily a moral rather than a political factor. The harm that is being done by foreign rule is seen by Seeley to be psychological. It represents a weakening of the mental and moral constitution. Independence becomes thus a necessity, if the moral fibre of Indian manhood and Indian womanhood is to be restored.

Mahatma Gandhi has constantly called this subservience, which is the result of long subjection, "slave mentality". The real problem calling for solution is the cost to character by which the protection of a foreign Government is being obtained. If it means the sacrifice of self-initiative in the governed, if it implies the inner weakening of the morale of those who are "protected", then the price is far too heavy. For this kind of debt has a strange way of mounting up, with its compound interest, until it is irretrievable. Bankruptcy of moral character follows as the inevitable result.

It is just at this point that Seeley's two historical maxims come in, towards which this long argument has been leading. The former of these two may be quoted in Seeley's own words as follows:—

> "Subjection for a long time to a foreign yoke is one of the most potent causes of national deterioration."

This sentence must not be regarded as the irresponsible utterance of a casual thinker. On the contrary, it is the historical judgment of one of the most careful and judicial historians of the nineteenth century. It has its own definite and immediate relation to the Indian problem. Every word of this closely packed sentence needs to be very carefully noted. Not every subjection, but subjection *for a long time*, to a foreign yoke is one of the most potent causes of national deterioration.

There are times in a people's history when the shock of a foreign dominion may bring life instead of death. Personally, as one who has made a special study of Indian history, I feel certain that there is much to be said for the belief that the shock of the Western impact upon the East, which came through the British connection, has brought new life with it to a remarkable degree. The great names in Indian history since the days of Raja Ram Mohan Roy represent a gallery of portraits of which any nation in the world may be proud. Compared with the eighteenth century, there can hardly be any question that the succeeding nineteenth century in India was an age of renaissance. The religious life of Hindu India received a marvellous inspiration, a new hope, and a new fulfilment. To take one instance only, the complete recovery of the Upanishad teaching stands out as a great landmark in the higher thinking of the human race. Islam also had its own revival. It shook itself free from an enslaving illiteracy. The ancient Syrian Christian Church of Malabar emerged from the slumber of ages as a caste-ridden community and sprang forward to new life. Missionary enterprise from without shook the whole social fabric of India. Hinduism was stirred to its depths in its reaction against this invasion of new ideas and set its own house in order. The ban of untouchability for the first time began to show signs of receding. Out of this very deep religious ferment, which was stirred up by the new leaven from the West, fresh vernacular literatures came to birth. The living languages of the people of India, which are employed in every day life, blossomed into song. The genius of art peculiar to India flourished in a thousand ways. Thus the nineteenth century in India had its own true greatness; and the shock from the West, however brutal in some of its forms, produced certain remarkable results in a quickened and creative life. To admit this is by no means to condone the methods whereby the subjection of India took place, or the ruthless and unscrupulous means that were employed in its accomplishment.

But at the same time, when the first quickening effects from foreign conquest had passed away, the evils that are inherent in such a system began to appear. The dead hand of external authority exercised from above proceeded to check and hinder the new living spiritual growth. The inevitable conflict between the inner spirit and external authority arose in an active form and has continued to increase ever since.

For the bad effect of foreign rule is this, that it can never assimilate itself to the growing needs of an awakening people. It is not immediately sensitive to new development and therefore proceeds to crush it. Thus it becomes repressive rather than responsive. The shock from abroad which gave life at one epoch, when prolonged beyond all endurance, brings death.

If we return to Seeley's historical maxim—that prolonged subjection to a foreign rule brings national deterioration—we can now see how true it is with regard to India. For since the British occupation began nearly two hundred years have passed and India is still ruled by foreigners. Every year that Indians still remain in subjection to Great Britain the moral and national deterioration must strike deeper. Therefore the question is being asked by every thinking Indian, "How much longer is India to continue in the world as a subject people? Is not every year that passes, while India still remains in subjection, only adding to the moral degradation?"

Here is the one hard, insoluble fact of current Indian history which has to be faced. According to Seeley's own verdict, for India to remain any longer in a state of subjection within the British Empire must lead to still further national deterioration. Something, therefore, must be done drastically before it is too late.

The second of the two historical maxims which Sir John Seeley puts forward is really the corollary of the former. It forces the Indian people into a still more intractable dilemma. For he faces frankly the ultimate question of the withdrawal of the British Government from India, and regards such a step as a well-nigh fatal calamity. In explaining his point he uses the following sentence, which has been one of the most frequently quoted from his book. He says:

> "To withdraw the British Government from a country like India, which has become dependent on it, and which we have made incapable of depending on anything else, would be the most inexcusable of all conceivable crimes and might cause the most stupendous of all conceivable calamities."

This relative clause, "which we have made incapable of depending on anything else," can have only one meaning. It implies that the British Government has made the Indian people so weak and defenceless that they have become unable to depend on their own resources if any occasion arose obliging them to offer their own defence against attack from outside. It implies also that no end to this weakening process is in sight. The British historian can look forward to no period wherein India will be able to depend on her own resources for her own protection.

"To withdraw the British Government from India,"

he says, "would be the most inexcusable of all conceivable crimes." Why is this? Because, to quote once more his fatal words, "we have made India incapable of depending on anything else". And again he writes as follows: "It is to be feared that the British rule may have diminished whatever little power of this sort India may have originally possessed".

I have quoted these blunt, harsh, and unpalatable sentences again and again because I want to drive home to the mind of the reader in the West what that deterioration means concerning which Sir John Seeley speaks in his earlier maxim. It shows the depth of humiliation that India has reached as a people by tamely submitting to a foreign yoke without making any strong united effort to throw off the subjection. Sir John Seeley himself was looking at the whole problem from a purely detached and scientific standpoint, as a curiously interesting phenomenon in human history. At the time of writing it did not intimately concern himself. But to Indians the question must necessarily be acutely personal. Just in proportion to the awakening of their national consciousness the humiliation of their own utterly dependent state will be felt.

Thus the necessary trend of events in India, according to this great historian, shows that she is becoming every year more and more helpless, more and more unable to evolve out of her own resources a stable form of government, more and more incapable of depending on anything else except the paramount British power. Nevertheless, this very course leads her downhill to the pit of destruction.

I can remember vividly even to-day how I went to Mr. Humphreys, the kindly Deputy Commissioner of Delhi, in the year 1907, at the time of Lala Lajpat Rai's arrest and imprisonment without trial, and protested that such an arrest without any trial was the surest way to drive Indians to despair. He used the very same argument as Seeley, and told me that it was necessary to do these harsh things, and treat Indians not as grown-up people but as wards of the British Government, because they had become so entirely helpless and defenceless that they must be protected even against themselves. The one thing that had to be observed at all cost in India was the Pax Britannica. Anything else would only result in the Pathans and Afridis and Afghans coming over the frontier and ruining the country. After all, law and order were of primary importance: all else was secondary.

This conversation with Mr. Humphreys almost drove me to despair at the time. He did not seem to realize that the very argument he was using was the greatest condemnation of British rule; for what could be more tragic than to make a whole people, who had once been so great and noble, entirely and utterly defenceless? Even if many blessings had been conferred, this was undoubtedly a curse. And yet in reality it was difficult at that time not to acknowledge the truth of what Mr. Humphreys had said. For Lord Morley's so-called liberal policy had brought with it very little salutary change. Even in the Civil Services practically all the chief responsible posts were still kept for Europeans. India was still a paternal despotism of an absolute character, ruled even in small details from Whitehall, seven thousand miles distant, and with no autonomous control. How far this autocratic rule had gone can hardly even be imagined in a free country like England, where things are so entirely different; or in Canada, where a career leading right up to the highest position of all is open to every man and every woman also. And I am afraid that an impartial historian would have to relate that national deterioration had been going on side by side with this sense of dependence. The two things have been almost interchangeable.

At last I, for one, have come to believe that, owing to the crushing military burden of a foreign army and a foreign civil service, the state of the peasantry, who have to pay the land tax in order to keep up this heavy expenditure, has grown recently worse instead of better. Meanwhile the lack of initiative and the sense of helplessness produced by foreign rule in the minds of the educated classes have led here also to a steady deterioration. Even such a conservative administrator as Sir Bamfylde Fuller has just written of a recent visit to Bengal, "In material prosperity I could see no signs of advancement among the common people. Villages and bazaars were still overhung by a cloud of poverty and squalor".

The rule of the British in India has often been regarded as parallel to that of the Roman Empire in ancient times, and there are many points at which the analogy holds good. But the parallel needs to be drawn out to its conclusion. The Romans built up a costly system of roads and walls, which were chiefly for strategic purposes. But when the Roman rulers were at last obliged to leave the shores of Britain the miserable inhabitants, who had become by slow degrees soft and defenceless under Roman protection, gazed longingly after their own conquerors as the Roman ships departed, carrying the troops away; for they had become too weakened by foreign protection to have any powers of self-defence left in them. History goes on to show how easily they succumbed to the more hardy invaders from the mainland of Europe who had not at any time been enervated by this protectionist Roman rule.

Thus we have reached in our argument, as we have followed closely Sir John Seeley's thesis, a position utterly intolerable to anyone who has self-respect. For Seeley appears to regard the people of India as having so entirely lost their powers of self-government and self-defence that in the end it would be nothing less than a crime of the worst character for Great Britain to leave them to themselves. This standpoint is taken again and again in *The Expansion of England* and it cannot possibly be treated lightly, as though it was of no historical importance. When seriously considered, it is in no sense whatever a thing to be proud of, that Great Britain has brought India into this false position. Even if the blame must be shared with the people of India themselves who were in such a state of weakness when the British entered India by sea and seized administrative power, this does not really diminish the blame that falls to the share of Great Britain. I will quote one other tragically illuminating passage from Seeley's *Expansion:*

> "India," he writes, "is of all countries that which is least capable of evolving out of itself a stable Government. *And it is to be feared that the British rule may have diminished whatever little power of this sort India may have originally possessed.*"

I have ventured to put this last sentence in italics, and surely it is a fatal confession for the English historian to make. If we think it out, it offers an altogether impossible prospect for a high-spirited people to contemplate. For it implies perpetual dependence, and subjection to the yoke of Great Britain.

Thus we have really come to a complete deadlock

in following out Sir John Seeley's closely reasoned argument. The situation is manifestly this, that if dependence and subjection to the foreign rule of the British Empire are to continue, then national deterioration is certain to continue with it. Yet if India struggles to be free and independent, then any withdrawal from her present position as a subject people becomes more and more unattainable in practice because the support and protection of Great Britain has become a perpetual necessity. The British rule has diminished "whatever little power of this sort India may have originally possessed".

In order to drive home the point before I turn to its remedy and to the method of India's recovery, let me give one other incident that happened while I was at Delhi and has been branded on my memory ever since. There had been at Aligarh a dispute between the students and the European staff. This had led to extreme bitterness. Then a sudden action on the part of the European Principal had provoked a college strike. The students refused to go back until their wrongs were righted. Early one morning at Delhi, Maulvi Nazir Ahmed and Munshi Zaka Ullah, whom I revered most deeply for their singular beauty of character, came to me, with tears in their eyes, to tell me that the Muhammadan Anglo-Oriental College at Aligarh, which was the one darling treasure of their hearts in their old age, was on the point of ruin. They asked me to come with them to Aligarh itself.

We went together and I could feel, without a word being said, the outraged spirit of the students—their resentment, their sense of humiliation, their feelings of injustice. During that very night, when we were present at Aligarh, it flamed forth in a literal deed. For the insulted students burnt their college furniture —their beds and mattresses, their tables and books. The flames mounted to the skies. They were a symbol of the student's own flaming indignation. After the strike was all over, and the students had gone back, and the disturbance was at an end, I asked from Maulvi Nazir Ahmed, what words of advice he had spoken to the students. He told me that he had said to them as follows: "You are slaves. What can slaves do? Get back to your books and work. You are not free men, but slaves".

These terrible words haunted me like an evil dream. Was that all the counsel he was able to give these young men at the very opening of their lives? Was that in very truth these students' true position? Were they slaves? The more I thought over it the more I found that the words had truth in them. This foreign subjection was a servitude of the soul, more insidious perhaps than any outward slavery, and none the less literally true.

CHAPTER VIII

THE VICIOUS CIRCLE BROKEN

Since this inescapable logic of Seeley with regard to the effect of foreign rule is not understood in the West and the sole blame for their own helpless condition is generally placed on Indians themselves, it has been necessary for me to labour the main argument of Seeley's book over and over again in order to drive home its serious implications. We can see from it that India has become by long subjection involved in a completely vicious circle. Whatever way we may turn in our argument, the fatal circle hems us in.

For many years after I had made my home in India and had become identified with her people this problem of her destiny remained with me as a hard, insoluble fact of daily life. Its brutally cold logic gripped my mind. Every day that passed I could see further into the grim reality of it; yet morally my whole soul revolted against such an intolerably weak conclusion, and I longed to find some way of breaking through the vicious circle itself in order to obtain release.

In this same connection, during this earlier period of my life in India the picture of some gradual development had attracted me, whereby power should be handed over little by little to the Indian people themselves with the necessary safeguards. These safeguards should ensure that the new powers shall be exercised aright. I could see that this ideal had been at the back of the minds of the best of my own fellow-countrymen from the very first.

Men like Elphinstone and Monro, Lawrence and Edwards, Ripon and Bright, had held it fast as an article of faith. The Queen's Proclamation of 1858 had made it a political principle, however far practice had fallen short and stultified it. The late Mr. G. K. Gokhale, who was one of the noblest statesmen India has ever produced, took up this same position of a gradual devolution of power, and he founded the "Servants of India Society" with this definite model in view. Regeneration of his country, he firmly believed, could not be attained amid a hurricane of political excitement, but only step by step. In such a gradual process it was of the essence of the solution of the problem to enlist the support of the British people by appeals to their better nature. He had no illusions as to the difficulties of the course to be pursued. He seemed to know them all beforehand; and yet his faith remained firm to the end, even after the heart-breaking experience of a Royal Commission which wasted the last years of his life by its futility.

But those who still hold this view, as I once held it in all sincerity, have to answer the problem of relativity, which is bound up with it. While time slips by further degeneracy is always taking place, and so the whole problem begins all over again. How can we get over the fact, which Seeley points out, that any further prolongation of British rule is certain to lead to fresh dependence and fresh degeneracy? The vicious circle is not escaped so easily as that.

Again, does not the old fatal leaning on Great Britain ruin everything? Is not this the very thing to be got rid of, if health is to return in the body politic? It is the old problem of "patronizing" the poor, only in another form. Anyone who has worked in a slum parish in London knows how harmful in the long run such patronizing from those who stand outside may become. My own experience in this direction at Walworth, in South-East London, stood me in good stead when I went to India. It made me profoundly distrust such paternal ways. It was easy to see that doles of Home Rule, meticulously meted out and rationed at the will of the rulers, could never create a new vital force within the soul. The "boon" theory simply did not work: it did more harm than good. Thus experience itself had already pointed out to me that this way of working out the problem in terms of gradual progress suffered from one defect. There was no inner strength in it, no inner resource whereby India might be rescued by her own efforts out of the evil that had hemmed her in on every side.

Desperate diseases demand desperate remedies and even at times require surgical operations. There is no permanent remedy in poultices when the centre of the disease is deep down within the body. Even if the outward dependence on Great Britain became slowly attenuated year by year, and different Reform Acts gave certain privileges and responsibilities which had not been offered before, nevertheless all these things would be a gift from without, an act of patronizing condescension. They would come within the scope of what I have called the "boon theory". Therefore, in respect to India, they would be a weakness rather than a strength to those who received them. In the interval, while these doles were being distributed and fought over, true independence would all the while be fatally undermined. The old evil habit of looking to Great Britain for everything in a defenceless sort of way would still remain. The internal disease which was the root of all the mischief would continue not merely uncured, but even more active than ever before.

Thus I came to realize by the force of sheer practical experience that the process of petitioning Great Britain and passively accepting whatever gifts or boons could be extracted from that quarter could not be at all relied on. Such an evolutionary remedy had one fatal flaw in it: it did not evolve. It only wandered round and round in a maze from which there was no way out. It therefore appeared to me practically certain that the only way of recovery was through some vital upheaval from within. The explosive force needed for such an internal upheaval must be generated within the soul of India itself. It could not come through concessions and proclamations.

At one time it appeared to me to be possible that the primitive Christian way of life might represent the one explosive inner force needed; and I still hold to this view of things, but in a form so profoundly changed as to represent almost a new discovery of Christ and a new interpretation of His way, about which I hope to write in due course. I had gone out to India originally in and through a missionary society—the Cambridge University Mission in Delhi. But I found in missionary efforts as they were carried on in India the conventional touch of a religious imperialism which had the same blighting effect on the inner self-determination of Indian Christians as the ordinary political imperialism had upon Indians who were not Christians. For where the Christian missionary effort came from the West it carried with it an atmosphere of unintentional patronage that was directly contrary to the way of life which Christ Himself taught and practised. Christ's whole spirit was that of meekness and lowliness of heart. He was ever by the side of the oppressed, and never by any stretch of imagination on the side of the oppressor. I could not recognize therefore in a "Church and Empire" creed any representation of the lowly Man of Nazareth, who suffered crucifixion at the hand of the authorities in Church and State alike. For ten years of long inner conflict I wrestled with this problem of conscience, until at last my freedom was won. Then I became a wanderer in the world, gladly entering into living touch with all those who would receive me, of whatever class or creed or religious faith. Not without a prolonged moral struggle was such independence realized; and it was the dynamic force of a great personal character, Rabindranath Tagore, entering at a critical moment into my life, that really carried me through. But the struggle served me in good stead. For it has enabled me to understand in a peculiarly sensitive manner something of what Indians themselves have individually experienced and suffered in their own struggle to gain release from external bondage. It also pointed the way to deliverance.

During these years, the pitiable condition of India, as a subject country, without any will of her own, weighed me down. I could see that those who had come from without, the British rulers, insisted on disposing India's destiny in their own dull, dogged way, whether Indians desired it or not. They were certain that they knew best and that Indians could not look after themselves. My whole soul revolted against this, and it seemed so utterly unfair and unjust to treat a highly intellectual people in this manner. The racial prejudice which I saw at work in conjunction with this superior air of domination shocked me even more deeply. It made confusion even worse confounded, and led to an isolation between the two races that was unnatural and inhuman. Yet at the same time it almost appeared that as an Englishman I could not avoid being a party to it all; this became a very great burden to me.

Therefore it kept coming into my mind to try to find a way out; and at first it was not easy to see what could be done. Then one day it was borne in upon me that I might somehow be able to help with regard to those Indians who had gone abroad into the British colonies and dominions; and here it was, in this new experience, that I saw with my own eyes the humiliating position of inferiority wherein Indian citizens were placed, and how at every turn they were suffering from injustice and unequal treatment. It was in Fiji and South Africa that the iron entered into my soul at the time when I went among the Indian settlers, who had originally gone out under a vicious system of labour called "indentured labour" and had received treatment which made racial equality unthinkable. They were known as "coolies" and treated in a subject manner. It was there also that for the first time I met Mahatma Gandhi. That meeting was to revolutionize and upset my own thinking as it has upset the thinking of many others since. Of one thing I have become at last convinced by the hardest logic of events—that unless Indians themselves are both morally and politically independent, the subjection which has gone so deep as to injure and deform the soul will never be removed. They will be treated still as "coolies" and not as free men.

All my life through I have been a student and a thinker and a reader of books, eager indeed at every turn to put thought to the test of action, but constitutionally unwilling and unfitted to take a leading part in such action except on very rare occasions. Wherever such occasions have arisen I have shrunk back as quickly as possible, because I have felt the political path to be something apart from my own. But I am now convinced, without any mental wavering or hesitation, that except complete independence, moral as well as political, is open for India to grasp with both hands she will never shake herself free from the subservience which has so enervated her. The vicious circle wherein she has become involved cannot otherwise be broken through.

On whichever side I look to-day, while considering the Indian future—on the side of trade and commerce; on the side of industry and labour; on the side of social reform and religious readjustment; on the side of literature, art and music—I can see the creative impulse sustained and the inward energy of the soul of the people responsive only when the moral standpoint of manly and womanly independence has been reached. I can see no creative life, but rather an enervated and enfeebled existence, if this perpetual dependence goes on, and if mere hobbling along with the help of crutches continues.

A Canadian, an Australian, can go wherever he pleases without asking "by your leave" from anyone. The world's charter of freedom is his. He is independent in every sense of the word. But an Indian is made to feel, wherever he goes, that he is restricted. Even in England itself restrictions bind him on every side, while in the Dominions he is not allowed even to land except on a ticket of leave. If he seeks residence he is politely refused. He is told that Australia is "white". In his own country itself his steps are dogged by the secret police if he has patriotic longings or if he becomes a member of a national congress organization. I have learnt by personal experience everything I have written down in this respect, and I know what this subjection means.

If this then has been my experience, bitter and deep, can it be realized with what intensity of relief I turned from this conservative process, which Mr. Gokhale stood for, to the sharp contrast of the volcanic personality of Mahatma Gandhi? For there had long seemed to be only one pathway which could lead out of this entangling dilemma and bring India release. If India could find, before it was too late, some God-given moral genius who could stir up, not in one province only, but throughout the whole country, the spirit of moral revolt and independence, then there might be some hope. If India could produce, out of her own store of inner resources, such an inspiring and unifying personality, then all might be well. But if no such religious and moral genius appeared, then

India's subjection, moral as well as physical, must go on interminably.

And surely this is just what has occurred, however disturbing the sudden event may be to our own conventional mode of thinking. For at this most critical time of all in Indian history, when subjection and dependence, outward and inward alike, were becoming no longer bearable or supportable, India has brought forth one of her own children who has uttered in his own way the words, "Be free: be slaves no longer!" and a new fearlessness has entered the heart. Men and women are ready, by their thousands, to go to prison for the sake of freedom. Instead of cringing to the dust they are holding their heads high. The Indian poet, Rabindranath Tagore, has proclaimed in an immortal poem this regenerating faith and purpose: "Where the head is held high and the mind is without fear. . . . Into that heaven of freedom, my Father, let my country awake". What the poet has sung and inspired, Mahatma Gandhi has put into action. The mind of India is without fear to-day and her head is held high among the nations.

It is true that with such a volcanic force as the personality of Mahatma Gandhi there is bound to be much destruction. Some pulling down will be witnessed before the building up can be seen. Prophets have always been men of strange, uncouth ways which shock our normal habits. We must expect that. But the essential factor after all is the new atmosphere, the new spirit, the new life-impulse from beneath, which has forced its way to the surface. This, in the end, will be creative instead of destructive. For this prophet of our own age, by himself living the life of fearlessness, has revealed to us all, and especially to his own people, the hidden power of a living freedom from within. He has taught us afresh, in new prophetic ways, the old lesson of prophecy of all ages, never to depend on external resources, or even on external authority, but upon ourselves. My heart has gone out along with that appeal, and I have a great hope that by setting out upon this pathway of inner freedom the full manhood and womanhood of independence will be reached in India at last.

So then it has been with the intense joy of mental and spiritual deliverance from an intolerable burden that I have watched in India the actual outburst of such an inner explosive force as that which occurred when Mahatma Gandhi spoke to the heart of India, not once or twice only, the releasing words "Be free!" and the heart of India responded. In a sudden moment her fetters began to be loosened, her subjection to disappear, and the pathway of freedom was opened.

In the atmosphere of gradual evolution such as Mr. Gokhale had outlined, I have had not one of my fundamental doubts answered. They offer palliatives rather than incisive remedies. They fail to reach the centre of India's deep-seated disease of "slave mentality". They only prolong the dependence of India on Great Britain. Along that line of advance there has been no vision before me of final deliverance. For the tragic fact always remains that independence becomes undermined as soon as ever it is built up.

But when I turn from this doubtful method of safeguarded reforms to the more direct treatment of Mahatma Gandhi, I can see that he cuts at the very roots of the disease. He is like a skilled surgeon performing an operation rather than a physician administering soothing drugs. And as his surgeon's knife cuts deep we can see at once the recovery of the patient beginning to take place—the recovery of self-respect, the regaining of true manhood and womanhood, the new spirit of independence.

But this freedom must be entirely unfettered; for in that lies its moral value. The independence must be unconditioned; for here again to impose conditions would destroy its moral content. That is the one lesson which has been taught by these continual struggles of non-co-operation. There can be no halfway house to loiter in while the struggle is going on. There can be no dallying in an intermediate stage where the great principles of freedom become confused and the swift currents of idealism run sluggish. Freedom rests ultimately in the mind. It is only by the exercise of freedom in the soul itself that new freedom can be won. The process is not unlike that of learning to walk when a child is young. The only way he learns is by constant falling and rising again from the ground. Every fall and every rise make the power of walking more perfect until the process itself becomes instinctive. So a protected India, with innumerable safeguards, can only develop weakness. But an India that launches out boldly into its own freedom under the inspiration of a moral genius like Mahatma Gandhi may fall back a hundred times, but in the long run it will stand upon its own feet with its manhood and womanhood restored to their full stature. No one but a prophet can bring to the heart of India in her present bondage the inward freedom which her soul so passionately desires.

CHAPTER IX

THE OLD LIBERAL IDEAL

After making this rapid survey of the fundamental conditions of the problem, with Sir John Seeley as our guide, it is necessary now to examine the whole position and groundwork afresh from a different angle. The chapters which follow will partly cover the ground which Seeley surveyed with such wonderful prescience. But while he only considered the foreign aspect of the British rule, as leading to internal weakness in India, what follows will deal rather with the relation between the two races, the Indian and the British, and the race friction that has been engendered. It will be seen from this new survey, when it is completed, that political relations between the two countries have here, also, come to such a pass and produced such a vicious circle of evil that the sooner the tension is relaxed and freedom from political domination is established the better.

It is obvious that this racial relation, with which the Simon Commissioners hardly deal at all, must vitally affect our judgment concerning the adequacy of their Report as a document of first importance. If there were no racial problem involved, things might still proceed gradually forward without serious inconvenience. But if every day the racial friction between the two countries must inevitably increase, then it is impossible to keep the decision of vital matters any longer in suspense. The strain must be relieved.

As we go over this new ground we can see that the constant racial treatment of Indians as subjects and inferiors has had in one important direction the stirring effect of a yeasty ferment. It has now leavened India through and through. For a distinct race consciousness has come up to the surface from within which cannot possibly be any longer suppressed. In a very definite sense this ferment that we are witnessing to-day must be regarded as a sign of new life and not of decay: it is surely preferable to the passive submissiveness of earlier bygone days. In its own way it may be called the partial fulfilment of what Macaulay and the liberal statesmen of the nineteenth century looked forward to as the goal of all their endeavours. For they had the courage and the wisdom to declare, as far back as a century ago, that it would be the proudest day in the annals of the history of Great Britain when India should gain her freedom.

But in all that they were attempting, early in the nineteenth century, they imagined a peaceful and not a hostile conclusion to the British occupation. They actually pictured to themselves, and Macaulay described in writing, a mutual friendship between the two countries growing ever closer and closer.[1] They

[1] Sir Henry Lawrence wrote in 1844, "Let us so conduct ourselves in our civil and military relations that, when the connexion between India and Great Britain ceases, it may do so, not with convulsions, but with mutual esteem and affection."

looked forward to a goodwill permanently and securely established even after independence had been reached. They did not put any trust in half measures, but had the fullest belief that freedom alone can produce freedom; that liberty is only gained by the exercise of liberty. Just as with a person learning the art of swimming, India had to make the plunge into liberty to learn the art of using it rightly. It may even still be possible that after the surging flood of national feeling in the younger generation has passed over, carrying the older people with it on its rising tide, this ancient foundation of goodwill and friendship, which our forefathers laid so well, will reappear above the surface of the current. But in what is happening to-day there is a note of hostility and bitterness which has not been heard before. This new portent should make the people of Great Britain pause in order to seek its remedy before it is too late.

Let us go back to Macaulay and the Reform Age in order to gain our lessons from it for the present time. Three remarkable steps were taken, during the years 1832 to 1834, which made that reform epoch a turning-point in the history of Great Britain. First of all there was the new charter of racial and religious equality in India, which was passed by Parliament in 1833. Secondly, the Abolition of Slavery throughout the British colonies followed a year later. Along with these two emancipating Acts, of the first importance, came the Reform Act itself, whereby the rotten boroughs were swept away and popular government in Britain was established through the extension of the franchise on a wide basis. The occasion was most critical; for civil war was not far distant. But in all three matters the British Parliament did the right thing at the right time.

It was a great blow to all that was happening in India and Great Britain that at such a unique time as this Raja Ram Mohan Roy, by far the noblest reformer of the age, should meet his death before his own work was fulfilled. But just before he died on September 27, 1833, he hailed the assured hope of these three reform measures as the beginning of a new dawn of freedom for mankind. To a much greater extent than any other figure, he stands out not only as the champion of immediate social reform, but also as the promoter of that union between East and West, which the liberal statesmen of England so ardently desired.

The builders of these foundations of human liberty, with the union of East and West as the end kept always in view, were a noble group of men. Raja Ram Mohan Roy, Dwarkanath Tagore, Macaulay, Lord Bentinck, Alexander Duff, are names that would be celebrated in any age. They built strong outworks of social justice and had faith in the fundamental principles of morality and religion. They held no narrow views of human life. One story may be told of Ram Mohan Roy which brings vividly before us his passionate love of freedom and his devotion to the whole human race, regardless of country or religion. When he broke through the last bonds of orthodoxy as a high-caste Brahmin, and made his adventurous sea voyage round the Cape of Good Hope, the East Indian merchantman on which he had sailed from Calcutta anchored safe from the storms in Cape Town harbour. Not far away from him was another ship, at whose mast-head floated the tricolour of France—the flag of the July Revolution by which despotism had been overthrown. In his eagerness to meet the officers who sailed under that flag of liberty, he asked for a boat to be lowered, that he might go aboard the French vessel in order to pay a tribute to the country which most of all had awakened freedom from its lethargy of ages. On his return to his own vessel an accident happened to him. He fell as he mounted the rope ladder and broke his leg. His own enthusiasm for France as the champion of human liberty never failed him. As he approached the shores of England he stated his intention, if the great Reform Acts were rejected by the British Parliament, to surrender his allegiance and retire to some country in his old age where liberty was honoured in deed as well as in word.

Men of outstanding moral genius such as Raja Ram Mohan Roy are rare in human history, and he left no immediate successor to carry on the work of binding India and Great Britain together in the common unity of mankind. But this ideal which he cherished has never been wholly lost sight of by the greatest Indian minds. It is the substance of Rabindranath Tagore's teaching to-day, and forms the basis of his own international university at Santiniketan. With Mahatma Gandhi also this true fellowship of man has been the final commanding principle which has animated him throughout his adventurous life. It stands always in the background of his autobiography, which he has called *Experiments with Truth*. Arabinda Ghose, the great recluse, has also preached it from his retirement.

The period of the Indian Mutiny need not be dealt with at any length, though it left long and bitter memories behind it.[1] In no sense was it a popular revolt, except in small areas of the country. It was crushed with a ruthlessness of vengeance which disgraced the name of a Christian Government, and this did far more harm to the cause of good will and mutual friendship than the bloodshed of the war itself.

But the basal fact of the supreme need of closer relations between India and Great Britain began to reassert itself among thoughtful educated people. The story of the life-work of Sir Syed Ahmad Khan, the Muhammadan leader, who founded the Anglo-Oriental College at Aligarh, illustrates this need from

[1] Professor E. J. Thompson's book *The Other Side of the Medal* has given for the first time a truthful documented narrative of what really took place. The accuracy of this book has never been challenged.

the side of Islam. He nobly overcame the resentment felt among the Musalmans in India, who had been made to suffer most after the Mutiny, and boldly grasped the hand of friendship that was offered from the British side. At Calcutta the meteoric figure of Brahmananda Keshub Chander Sen shone out brilliantly for a time, and his magnetic personality attracted the West towards the East as no other individual had done since Raja Ram Mohan Roy. In a book which I have recently written, called *Zaka Ullah of Delhi*,[1] I have tried to draw, with a full historical background, the picture of those times when India and Great Britain very gradually drew together in sympathy once more after the dark episode of the Mutiny was over. In that book it was my one object to show how fruitful this genuine meeting of East and West might become. For in Munshi Zaka Ullah of Delhi there was an almost perfect example of Eastern courtesy and learning, and at the same time a liberal outlook upon the West, with an ardent search for truth and wisdom wherever it could be found. Nothing, it appeared to me, could be more important at the present time than the study of such outstanding characters in India, which win our reverence and love.

Perhaps the greatest opportunity of cementing this revival of mutual good will between India and Britain, after the Mutiny had been forgotten, came to the

[1] *Zaka Ullah of Delhi*, by C. F. Andrews, published by W. Heffer & Son, Ltd., Cambridge, 1929.

British people during the last thirty years of the nineteenth century. For during those eventful and constructive years there was only a comparatively small group of Indian students coming over to study in this country; but among these were young men of brilliant promise, who were certain to rise to eminence in their own society after they had returned. The Universities of Oxford and Cambridge, together with the medical and law schools at Edinburgh and London, were the chief centres of learning to which they went for their studies. The affection from their side, which they were ready to offer, was lavish and open-hearted, if only there had been those on the British side ready to respond to it.

Rabindranath Tagore and Mohandas Gandhi, who were both at different intervals in London during those crucial years, have told us the story of their own loneliness in that vast modern city. Tagore, who was only seventeen years old when he came over from Calcutta in 1878, was shy and self-diffident; Gandhi, who arrived about ten years later, was equally retiring. Though they have both acknowledged small kindnesses done to them by humble, unknown English men and women, it is easy to trace in their writings the misery of isolation from which they suffered in a strange land. Some deeper touch of human sympathy might have done much for them at such a desolate time. But their experience in England was in this respect very disappointing.

Yet in spite of all this, however dull, unimaginative and insular our home folk may have been in those days—and on this side the British people have an obvious weakness—there was not as yet any race or colour prejudice. On the contrary, there was a high sense of human freedom and a great liberal tradition. In Tagore's and Gandhi's own descriptions of their early life in London there is no mention at all of any bad racial treatment. That point never comes up. Insulting questions about race and colour were then practically unknown in England. It was a land of racial justice, and its ideals of political democracy were highly regarded by them in their younger days.

One thing further needs to be made clear. Every student from India throughout this period owed a great debt to English literature. The love of freedom which runs through the English poets kindled their youthful imaginations. Scott and Dickens, Shakespeare and Milton, Shelley and Wordsworth, were all of them household names, loved and cherished as their very own. The Bible also, as great literature, was widely read and admired.

It is easy for me vividly to recall the genuine delight shown by the elder brother of Rabindranath Tagore, even in his extreme old age, whenever he quoted from his favourite English authors. He had a simple, child-like nature. A more guileless and innocent old man it would have been impossible to meet. He was affectionately called by everyone alike, Borodada.[1] Although

[1] Elder Brother.

he was a very great philosopher and sage, deeply revered, the little children loved him as one of themselves and made friends with him at first sight. Even the birds and squirrels would come and eat from his plate, or from his hand, as he sat on the veranda. As a follower and disciple of Mahatma Gandhi, he was an ardent non-co-operator. Thus he was politically opposed to the British Government, and in his own way even in his old age a fiery patriot. But, all the same, the English poets were very dear to him indeed. He never wished to non-co-operate with them or to boycott them. While reading their pages he still looked upon Great Britain with the old kindly eyes of a deep affection. He had a special love for Scotland, because of his romantic devotion to Sir Walter Scott as a storyteller. But Shakespeare was to him the greatest author that England had ever produced, and even when non-co-operating he looked upon England through Shakespeare's eyes.

Up to this point in my argument it will be seen that Macaulay's ideal still held its own place in the historical development of India, chiefly because it was based on the truth, and therefore could not be wholly shaken, even though for a time the two countries, India and Great Britain, fell apart or came into conflict with each other. The need of India for the new life and culture of the West and the need of Great Britain for the material support and spiritual ideas which India could give from her Eastern standpoint helped to restore the link as soon as it was broken. During the last quarter of the nineteenth century, owing chiefly to Max Müller's remarkable work at Oxford, the greatness of Eastern civilization, and especially of Indian culture, became acknowledged by all right-thinking men. The advent of Swami Vivekananda to the West completed this remarkable triumph of Eastern thought, which Raja Ram Mohan Roy and Keshub Chander Sen had begun. The West for the first time in all its historical development, since the dawn of Christianity, began to look through Eastern eyes at mankind and the universe. It would almost seem as though intellectual fellowship would cement those bonds of good will between India and Great Britain for which the great liberal statesmen of England had so ardently striven.

CHAPTER X

THE NEW RACIAL FACTOR

Even up to the recent era of the World War this sentiment of British liberty and justice remained quite strong in the minds of the older generation in India.[1] It had never hitherto been seriously challenged by directly contrary facts. This accounts for the generous response to Great Britain's appeal to all Indians to take their part in the European War side by side with the British troops when Belgium was invaded. In those early days of the World War that conflict was regarded as the battle for human freedom against the militarism of the Central Powers.

Rabindranath Tagore, though opposed on principle to war as inhuman, at first took up that position himself with regard to the invasion of Belgium, considering it a grave injustice. He told me at the very time how he had Belgium in his mind when he wrote his celebrated poem, called *The Boatman*, wherein he pictures a lonely, desolate woman sitting in solitude beside her vanished home. Mahatma Gandhi also believed in the justice of the Allied cause, and offered again and again for active service as the organizer of an ambulance corps. He sustained this belief in the sincerity of the Allies right up to the end.

But when towards the close of the war the shameful

[1] See Appendix I.

treaties secretly made between the Allied Powers were brought to light, dividing the spoils, the more sordid aspect of the struggle became only too evident. This bargaining away of human lives for power, among those who professed themselves openly to be champions of freedom, immediately brought with it a blow to that confidence in the justice of the British cause which had hitherto been almost unchallenged. At his request I went with Mahatma Gandhi to the War Conference in Delhi early in May, 1918, when the situation appeared most critical on both the Eastern and Western fronts, and there was some danger of the invasion of India from the north. Just before I reached Delhi I received by mail a copy of the *Nation* giving the full text of the secret treaties. This staggered me, and I showed it at once to Mahatma Gandhi. He went with it forthwith to the Viceroy, Lord Chelmsford. The Viceroy told him that the genuineness of the documents was not yet proven, and that meanwhile it was necessary to get on with the war. Mahatma Gandhi accepted the Viceroy's position for the time being, but when afterwards the genuine character of the treaties was proved the shock of disillusionment was all the greater.

Other shocks of the same kind followed. Germany was made to accept the Armistice on the ostensible basis of President Wilson's Fourteen Points; but when she was utterly defenceless, this basis was altered to the enforced signing of the most humiliating treaty ever offered to a great nation. This came as another terrible blow to the faith of Indian leaders in the righteousness of the Allied cause. Later still, one act followed another, disclosing the brutality of war itself in different ways. The name of Great Britain was dragged in the dust by crooked diplomacy, broken promises, and cynical appeals to force and force alone, as the one final arbiter between nations. The tragedy of Ireland added to the moral confusion. The climax of disillusionment came when a widely circulated book, disclosing the most flagrant falsehoods of British war propaganda and openly boasting of their cleverness, was read and quoted in India. After that, it was difficult to maintain any credit for honour or integrity on the part of the belligerents.

It has been necessary to recall these sordid things, which should otherwise be forgotten, because they have a very direct relation to the universal lack of trust which is felt in India towards Great Britain at the present time. They partly account for it and explain it. To those of us who were in India after the Armistice, during those months of war exhaustion and moral bankruptcy, it was a hard matter indeed to find out each moment how to act, how to speak, and what to leave undone and unsaid. For one moral principle after another was being surrendered by the Government in power in Great Britain.

But the worst has yet to be told. For out of the same war mentality came the shooting in Jallianwala Bagh at Amritsar, and the "crawling order". These military excesses, and those that followed in the Punjab villages under martial law, represented an almost unbelievable lapse from what had always been regarded in India as a British standard of justice. They showed the old evil spirit still lingering on after the war was over.

During these grim days, when brute force was allowed to break loose unchecked, I was present in Delhi; and later on in the Punjab I tried to enter the martial law area itself, but was deported. Also I was with the poet Rabindranath Tagore when he wrote his famous letter surrendering his knighthood. The mental agony that he suffered before he wrote that letter few can understand. Never in all my life have I passed through darker times than those. It seemed as though the whole moral fabric of society had been rent in twain by an earthquake shock.

If we look carefully away from all the moral confusion of those times, in order to discover the exact point of stress where the final breach came and the gulf yawned widest, we shall see it most clearly in the racial arrogance with which Europe faced the East. Great Britain in particular, along with the British Dominions, was in this regard the worst offender. The "crawling order" at Amritsar, already mentioned, had its poisonous stab in the fact that it was racial. It was a brutal expression, brutally devised, of racial superiority enforced by military power. Its direct counterpart in a different sphere was seen in the League of

Nations itself, when the way was finally blocked to the acceptance of Japan's resolution that racial equality should be included as one of the underlying principles of the Covenant of the League. This, when combined with the "white" policy of Australia and Canada, and the hard, intransigent racialism of South Africa and Kenya, has made it exceedingly difficult for Indians who have any self-respect to remain in a Commonwealth that has really become a "white race" Empire. It is here, therefore, on this question of offensive racial treatment exercised upon an acutely sensitive people that the spirit of India has been most passionately stirred to open revolt. It is here also that almost every single educated Indian has had some painfully bitter personal insult to bear in his own life, owing to some racial incident happening to him in his own country at the hand of Europeans. For it has to be confessed with shame that in India itself the very same race prejudice is now present which we find in Kenya and South Africa. The form it takes may be less aggravated to-day, but the spirit of racial insolence survives.[1]

If the argument be used that in spite of all these untoward circumstances (which were mainly due to the brutality of war conditions) Great Britain showed her own good will to India in the Government of India

[1] See Lieutenant-Colonel Osburn, D.S.O., *Must We Lose India?*, page 17. The whole book tells the same story at first hand.

Act, of 1919–1921, whereby a reformed constitution of a liberal character was granted to India by Great Britain, and that no gratitude, but only ingratitude, was offered for such a signal boon, there are many answers which may be made from the Indian side.

First of all, the "boon" theory, as I have already written, can never be accepted in India. "Swaraj (self-government) is my birthright" has been all along the motto of the national movement; and for the British to speak of "boons" is only to rouse useless irritation.

Secondly, the Government of India Reform Act was an altogether half-hearted affair, based on the safeguarding of certain reserved subjects by keeping them strictly in official hands, that is to say, under British control. Everyone, including the Simon Commissioners, has agreed that this Dyarchy (as it was called) was unworkable. The Commissioners have therefore recommended that it should immediately be abandoned. For this reason there is no need to discuss it in this book. All that can be said in its favour has been well said in the Simon Report.

Mahatma Gandhi has been widely regarded in Great Britain as unreasonable in his political demands. Yet even after the shooting at Amritsar in April 1919 he proposed and carried with great difficulty at the National Congress of December 1919, when public national feeling was at its highest pitch of excitement, the acceptance of the Government of India Reform

Act with a promise to work it with good will. He did this in spite of the fact that the majority of the Congress members were insistently demanding a boycott. He only carried this resolution for the acceptance of the Reform Act by the sheer weight of his moral personality. He actually got the National Congress to promise to try to work a constitution, the abandonment of which, as unworkable, has now been recommended by the Simon Commissioners.

But after he had won this personal victory, the events of 1920—the half-hearted condemnation of General Dyer by the Hunter Commission, the actual condonation of his disgraceful act by the House of Lords, the breach of promise to the Turks by Mr. Lloyd George—filled the cup of racial injustice to the full. Every thinking Indian felt that Great Britain had determined to favour her own race, even when it was in the wrong, and to keep India in racial subjection. For these reasons it was decided at last to non-co-operate, and the non-co-operation movement was started.

After Mahatma Gandhi's release from prison in 1924, which was followed by the gentle goodness of the doctors and nurses while he was ill at Poona, a kindlier human feeling grew up on both sides, and there seemed every prospect of a reconciliation. But the perpetual racial friction—now in Kenya, now in South Africa, and yet again suddenly arising through some flagrant act of racial injustice elsewhere—exacerbated the situation. A partial victory was gained in South Africa over some of the worst race prejudice in the world, owing to the winning and gracious personality of Srinavasa Sastri, whose pure human good will worked a miracle in that sub-continent. But the world trend of recent events has on the whole swung backwards rather than forwards.

The most alarming feature of all is the undoubted fact that in Great Britain itself, where before there was hardly a sign of such an evil, the sudden ebullition of a race superiority complex has appeared on the surface of our social life which forebodes nothing but evil. When I have been in the company of Indian students in London and elsewhere I have been frequently told about this change of temper. What is sometimes called the "South African point of view" on the race question has been steadily gaining ground and making new converts. It has been the post-war mind, realistic and cynical, which has given it a foundation. It has penetrated the old Universities of Oxford and Cambridge, and has found an unwholesome lodgement in Edinburgh and London.

Those Indian residents in this country who have been here for a long while have explained to me quite frankly that the more recent years since the World War have been the worst of all. In conversation with me they have often ascribed this development to the war itself and the brutalities which the war engendered. When I have heard from their own lips stories, faithfully told, concerning personal incidents which have happened to themselves it has been hard to realize that in Britain, which had prided herself hitherto on her freedom from race and colour prejudice, such a profound change could have come about so suddenly and with so little care being taken to check it at its first onset directly after the war. I have been assured by Indians themselves that when simple hotel accommodation is needed by them, or even a simple meal at a public restaurant, sometimes the greatest difficulty is now experienced where in earlier years there would have been no difficulty at all. Distinguished Indians, whose names I know well but refrain from mentioning for obvious reasons, have thus been insulted. The gentlest people in the world and the most courteous have been thus rudely refused.

All this would have been quite incredible to me in Great Britain before the European War, and it remains still very nearly unthinkable to-day, even though I have seen elsewhere what evil the war spirit could effect. But the facts, I am afraid, are now quite indisputable, for I have tested them thoroughly. The further I have gone into the matter the more disastrous the outlook has appeared for the future.

It is now evident to me, and it seems to me necessary openly to state it, that entirely new opinions are being formed in this country on those crucial racial issues which most of all divide Great Britain and India. These new ideas, crudely formed but doggedly held, absolutely reject equality. They would thus make finally impossible any intimate friendly relation, within the same Commonwealth, of Indian and British people. They would imply perpetual subjection of one race to another. That same good will on equal terms which Macaulay contemplated a century ago is now definitely denied to Indians by many of Macaulay's fellow-countrymen.

With regard to these very startling developments, which are of comparatively recent growth in Great Britain, the churches in this country appear to give as yet only a timid and uncertain moral guidance. The elder statesmen of the British Commonwealth likewise hesitate when any direct issue is brought forward at an Imperial Conference. Yet it ought to be self-evident that upon this one issue, as far as India is concerned, there can be no compromise and no prevarication. There can be no playing fast and loose either in Church or State. A plain answer, yes or no, must be given to a plain question.

What I have written may appear at first sight to have wandered far afield from the constitution-making character of the Simon Report as it looks out upon the future of India. But in reality every word of it is wrapped up with the main question, because one of the issues to be settled in the proposals which the Commissioners make is what place the British themselves should occupy in the scheme of things during the time of transition. And this depends entirely on whether they are racially acceptable or racially not acceptable to the Indian people. If on account of increasing racial friction they are unacceptable, then, to put it bluntly, the sooner they retire the better. For, as Seeley has shown, it is the stupidest thing in the world that England should ever think that she can keep India within the British Empire by force. Die-hards of that temper who retain any such idea in their heads are suffering from a mental hallucination.

If on the other hand the racial friction dies down and equality of status is in every sense of the word actively and openly acknowledged both in India and in Great Britain, then the whole question of the length of time required for transference of responsibility to Indian hands becomes much simpler. Mahatma Gandhi has said repeatedly that if a "change of heart" took place in the rulers he for one would welcome their presence in his own country as ministers and servants; but he would not have them remain a single day longer in the position of arrogant masters.

CHAPTER XI

EAST AND WEST

There is one sonnet written by Michael Drayton in the great Elizabethan period of English literature that has often appealed to me as representing by analogy the strained relationship between England and India, which is to-day a part of the great controversy between East and West.

What student of human history can fail to remember the earlier days of last century, which I have recalled, when the West with its new liberty ushered in by the French Revolution was idealised by the greatest thinkers of the East? A generous, whole-hearted friendship, bordering on devoted love, was then offered freely to the West by the East. Men like Ram Mohan Roy and Keshub Chander Sen poured out their eloquent admiration in words that seem almost extravagant as we read them to-day. The West was to be the great Emancipator of the human race from every form of bondage!

But gradually, as the century advanced, the greed of material things and the ambition for fresh fields of conquest began to poison, like a canker in the bud, this incipient friendship. The East, disappointed and disillusioned, lost its earlier glow of enthusiasm. The bitterness of subjection took the place of the earlier rejoicing. The cold disdain of the West cut at the roots of the old affection and made its foliage wither. The twentieth century has witnessed a still further encroaching of this haughty superiority of the West, with its rejection of any advance made towards equality. The hand of equal friendship offered by the East is rejected. At last the cry is raised:—

> Since there's no help come let us kiss and part,—
> Nay I have done, you get no more of me;
> And I am glad, yea, glad with all my heart
> That thus so cleanly I myself can free.
> Shake hands for ever, cancel all our vows,
> And when we meet at any time again,
> Be it not seen in either of our brows
> That we one jot of former love retain.

The solemn monosyllables of these opening lines, like the tolling of a funeral bell, usher in the last six lines of the sonnet, where the disdain, in return for disdain, is broken by one last appeal. The majestic music passes on to its great conclusion:—

> Now at the last gasp of Love's latest breath,
> When, his pulse failing, Passion speechless lies
> When Faith is kneeling by his bed of death
> And Innocence is closing up his eyes,
> Now if thou would'st, when all have given him over
> From death to life thou might'st him yet recover.

Is it too much to hope that the last stanza may yet come true, and that at this last hour love's friendship based on true equality may return?

The issues are so vast that the world-hope for humanity seems to depend upon this one factor.

Nothing could be worse for mankind than the state of things to-day, where the West insists on treating the East as racially inferior and in a lower grade of civilization. No possible hope can come to fruition until this intolerable racial arrogance is abandoned. It is necessary to say this openly and without any qualification.

But even after all this is acknowledged to the full much still remains to be done, and the step forward to meet the East must now come from the West; for it denotes a change of heart which to many at first sight will seem unpractical. In the end, however, it may be found not impossible to accomplish.

The change is expressed in Christ's words which I have taken as a motto for this book: "The kings of the Gentiles do exercise lordship over them, and they that have authority over them are called Benefactors. But it shall not be so with you: but he that is greater among you let him be as the younger. . . . For I am among you as he that serveth".

Is it possible to change the position of the British in India from that of lordship to that of service? The Anglo-Indian, as he was called, in the old days, was proud to be called Benefactor: but this went with a "lordship" which now must be entirely abandoned. Let me repeat the vital fact that Mahatma Gandhi himself has said that he has no wish to get rid of a single Englishman from India, if only he is willing to remain and serve instead of ruling. Since

Gandhi uttered those words, he has never withdrawn them; and the principle of Ahimsa (or loving-kindness) which lies behind them is so fundamental with him that they may be said to form a part of his own inner spirit. Is it not possible in practice to realize such a change as this? Already in Iraq a half-way-house to this position of service has been discovered, which may illustrate what I mean. Under the new Treaty, Englishmen are to remain in an advisory capacity without any authoritative powers. The Government of Iraq is to use their counsel in this subsidiary manner. Something even further will be needed in India. There will be required in the future men and women from this country, or from any other Western nation, who will regard it as their greatest privilege in life to serve under Indians instead of directing them or ruling over them.

The English correspondent from Bombay whom I have already quoted in this volume[1] writes: "As an Englishman I pray that we may rise to great heights." Personally, I have faith enough in my own fellow-countrymen to know that such an appeal as this is not impossible of realization. About the Indians themselves this correspondent has written: "When men get to the state of delighting to go to prison for their convictions, then it is time something was done". On the moral plane, the Indian national volunteers have already risen to great heights. They have displayed an

[1] See chapter ii, p. 42.

amazing moral fortitude. Surely the true meeting of East and West can be brought about on that plane! The often misquoted lines about the twain never meeting have this proviso added, that where two strong men meet face to face there is neither East nor West, but only a common humanity and a common respect for each other. The poet wrote those lines of his about physical strength; and it is quite easy for the Englishman and the Pathan to respect that kind of courage. But what is needed from either side now is to respect a moral courage that requires far greater nerve than mere physical prowess. If the Englishman is able to show the moral courage of meekness and humility; if the Indian is able to show the moral courage of high fortitude and manly suffering without striking a blow; then, by rising to such heights as these, a higher friendship may be engendered. It will not be the old patronising friendship of the nineteenth century, but the equal friendship of the twentieth. It will mean that rare brotherhood and sisterhood which Walt Whitman has called "the dear love of comrades".[1]

[1] See Appendix VII and also V.

APPENDICES

Since it is important to understand sympathetically what the greatest Indian minds are thinking concerning the present situation, I have given here at some length two recent statements by Tagore and two others by Gandhi. They will throw much light on all that I have written.

C. F. A.

APPENDIX I

INTERVIEW WITH RABINDRANATH TAGORE

An interview was given to the *Manchester Guardian* by the poet Rabindranath Tagore, on Saturday, May 17, 1930. The poet said as follows:—

"When I was young, we were all full of admiration for Europe, with its high civilization and its vast scientific progress, and especially for England, which had brought this civilization to our own doors. We had come to know England through her glorious literature, which had brought a new inspiration into our young lives. The English authors, whose books and poems we studied, were full of love for humanity, justice, and freedom.

"This great literary tradition had come down from the Revolution period. We felt its power in Wordsworth's sonnets about human liberty. We gloried in it even in the immature productions of Shelley, written in the enthusiasm of his own youth, when he declared against the tyranny of priestcrafts and preached the overthrow of all despotisms through the power of suffering bravely endured.

"All this fired our own youthful imaginations. We believed with all our simple faith that even if we rebelled against foreign rule we should have the sympathy of the West. We felt that England was on our side in wishing us to gain our freedom.

"But during the interval that followed there came a rude awakening as to our actual relations. We found them at last to be those of force rather than freedom. This not only disturbed in a great measure our youthful dream; it also began to shatter our high idea concerning our English rulers themselves. We came to know at close quarters the Western mentality in its unscrupulous aspect of exploitation, and it revolted us more and more. During the present century, and especially since the European War, this evil seems to have grown still worse, and our bitterness of heart has increased.

"Those who live in England, away from the East, have now got to recognize that Europe has completely lost her former moral prestige in Asia. She is no longer regarded as the champion throughout the world of fair dealing and the exponent of high principle, but rather as the upholder of Western race supremacy and the exploiter of those outside her own borders.

"For Europe it is, in actual fact, a great moral defeat that has happened. Even though Asia is still physically weak and unable to protect herself from aggression where her vital interests are menaced, nevertheless, she can now afford to look down on Europe where before she looked up.

"This new strained mental attitude carries with it tragic possibilities of long-continued conflict. The European nations, dimly realizing the danger of this growing alienation, still only think of artificial readjustments through various mechanical means. They merely talk of possibilities of the big Powers themselves combining for united action, forgetful of the fact that these very Powers are daily destroying world peace, for in their racial pride they altogether ignore the East. They do not realize that their blindness of arrogance and insistence on their own superiority must sooner or later involve both hemispheres in ruin.

"In face of all this, which has become more and more apparent to me as I have grown old, I have often been asked in England to offer my opinion about what should be done at the present juncture when things have become so critical. My answer has always been that I do not believe in any external remedy where inner relations have been so deeply affected. For this reason, I cannot truly point to any short cut to win relief, or any easy remedy to heal the deep-seated disease. What is most needed is rather a radical change of mind and will and heart.

"What I really believe in is a meeting between

the best minds of the East and the West in order to come to a frank and honourable understanding. If once such an open channel of communication could be cut whereby sincere thought might flow freely between us, unobstructed by mutual jealousy and suspicion and unimpeded by self-interest and racial pride, then a reconciliation might be bridged over.

"Meanwhile, let it be clearly understood in the West that we who are born in the East still acknowledge in our heart of hearts the greatness of the European civilization. Even when in our weakness and humiliation we aggressively try to deny this we still inwardly accept it. The younger generation of the East, in spite of its bitterness of soul, is eager to learn from the West, and to assimilate the best that Europe has to offer. Even in our futile attempts to sever our connection with the West, while we struggle for political freedom, we are really paying the West the highest compliment we can offer. For we acknowledge in the very act of striving for liberty the noble character of the Western education which has roused us from our slumbers. We tacitly admit that it was the literature of the West which inspired us with a courageous love of freedom and aroused us to proclaim our independence.

"The comparative immunity which we enjoyed in the past, together with large powers of freedom of speech—all this quickened our courage and kept us free within. It should, therefore, be the anxious care as well as the proud privilege of Britain to maintain and foster the encouragement of that freedom. In spite of the trouble in which we are all involved at the present moment, England has to show herself broad-minded, upright, and conciliatory in her dealings with India to-day.

"For it must be clearly understood in England that complications have now arisen which can never be done away with by repression and by a violent display of physical power. They can only be cured by some real greatness of heart which will attract in its turn a genuine spirit of co-operation from our side. Those who have experience of bureaucratic and irresponsible Governments can easily understand how the repressive measures which are being undertaken to-day, culminating in martial law at Sholapur, are bound to react upon our own people, for fear and panic always make a Government in power harsh and vindictive. Instances of this are well known in human history, and what is happening to-day in India is not likely to be an exception to the general rule. . . .

"The time will come when reparation will have to be made. Therefore, I trust and hope that the best minds of England will feel ashamed of every form of tyrannical action, just as we ourselves have been ashamed at the violence which has broken out on our side. We must on no account, if we can help it, find ourselves involved in a vicious circle wherein one violence leads on to another. For that in the end can only lead on to further bitterness and estrangement."

APPENDIX II

TAGORE'S MESSAGE TO THE SOCIETY OF FRIENDS

The following is the substance of the message given by Rabindranath Tagore at the Yearly Meeting, in the Friends' House, London, on May 24, 1930:—

"India is being ruled by a complicated machine. The mechanics who drive it have a long training in power, but no tradition of human sympathy, which is superfluous in a workshop. They are incapable of understanding the living India owing to the natural mentality of bureaucracy, which simplifies its task and manages an alien race from a distance through various switches and handles and wheels and hardly ever through human touch. It produces perfect results so long as the subject race meekly behaves like dead material yielding to the machine-made law and order, offering no resistance when exploited. The people morally responsible for this flawlessly standardized rule lives across a far-away sea, satisfied at the unmurmuring silence brooding over a vast country—at a peace which is uncreative like that of a barren waste—and clings to a comfortable faith in the man on the spot and to the proud privilege of a first-class power in the West.

"In the meanwhile Europe's own quickening

touch has gradually awakened the dormant life of India. But the machine manufactured over a century ago, in its stolid indifference still ignores it, and in a blind insensitive efficiency tries to make mincemeat of the newly risen humanity of India; for alas, it knows nothing better. The expert in the engine-room is indignant to find that the time-honoured system no longer produces law and order, and he becomes more and more red in the face and dangerously furious.

"What Mahatma Gandhi had tried to do was to request the expert not to identify himself completely with the machine, but to remember that he is also a man. For the sake of his human dignity he must not offer a stone to the other man who is famished for bread, and blows when he claims self-respect. This was asked not merely because it is not human, but also because it can never work.

"I know at this moment there are thousands in my country who are suffering without any chance of redress, even those who do not deserve it. For the machine-government lets loose its fury of wholesale suspicion against risks which its blindness cannot define. But I hate to indulge in self-pity on an occasion like this. Conflicts between man and the machine have often happened in various shapes in human history. It is a desperate struggle, and man defeats the machine not always by his success but by his sufferings.

"I deliberately use the word machine, for it is not your great people who is behind this fight. I myself have a firm faith in what is human in your nation, and the credit is yours for this very struggle for freedom that has been made possible to-day in India. The courage that has been aroused in our country—the courage to suffer—carries an unconscious admiration for your own people in its very challenge. For it cannot be a desperately physical challenge that madly rushes to an utter suicide in fighting against odds. At heart it is a moral challenge, being sure of a moral response in your mind when our claim is made real to you by our sufferings. Such sufferings have won your admiration. You secretly feel small by the enormities that you allow to be perpetrated in a state of panic upon a people who are no match for you in their power to return your blows adequately or retaliate your insults; for you cannot belie your real nature and all that has made you great. Being sure of it, Mahatma Gandhi had the temerity to ask you to take our side and help us to gain the greatest of all human rights, freedom, and to free yourself from the one-sided relationship of exploitation, which is parasitism, surely causing gradual degeneration in your people without your knowing it.

"I have been asked whether we must have complete independence. In answer I say that there can be no absolute independence for man. Interdependence is in his nature and it is his highest goal. All that is best in humanity has been achieved by mutual exchange of minds among peoples that are far apart, and is ever waiting for mutual enjoyment. This spirit must also come over man's politics, which for want of it is poisoned by envy and hatred and enveloped in a noxious atmosphere of falsehood and campaign of calumny, menacing peace at the least provocation. Let the best minds of the East and West join hands and establish a truly human bond of interdependence between England and India in which their interests may never clash, and they may gain an abiding strength of life through a spirit of mutual service without having to bear a perpetual burden of slavery on one side and a diseased responsibility on the other which is demoralizing.

"In its relation to the eastern peoples the aspect of western character which has come uppermost is not only insulting to us but to the West itself. Nothing could have been more unfortunate in the history of man than this. For all meetings of men should reveal some great truth which is worthy of a permanent memorial, such as, for instance, had been the case of India's meeting with China in the ancient time.

"At the moment when the West came to our door, the whole of Asia was asleep, the darkness of night had fallen over her life. Her lights were dim, her voice mute. She had stored up in her vaults her treasure, no longer growing. She had her wisdom shut in her books. She was not producing living thoughts or fresh forms of beauty. She was not moving forward but endlessly revolving round her past. She was not ready to receive the West in all her majesty of soul. The best in us attracts the best in others: our weakness attracts violence to our neighbourhood, as thinness in the air attracts a storm. To remain in the fulness of our manifestation is our duty, not only to ourselves but for others. We have not seen the great in the West because we have failed to bring out the great that we have in ourselves, and we are deluded into thinking that we can hide this deficiency behind borrowed feathers. This is the reason why we claim freedom in order to find a real basis for interdependence. The usual form of spiritual expression that we find in the lives of the best individuals in western countries is their love of humanity, their spirit working through their character; their keen intellect and their indomitable will leagued together for human welfare. In their individuals it reveals itself in loyalty to the cause of truth for which so many of them are ready to suffer martyrdom, often standing heroically alone against some fury of national insanity. When their wide human interest, which is intellectual, takes a moral direction, it grows into a fulness of intelligent service of man that can ignore all geographical limits and racial habits of tradition.

"But what is most unfortunate for us in Asia is the fact that the advent of the West into our continent has been accompanied not only by science, which is truth and therefore welcome, but by an impious use of truth for the violent purpose of self-seeking which converts it into a disruptive force. It is producing in the countries with which it is in contact a diseased mentality that refuses moral ideals, considering them to be unworthy of those who aspire to be rulers of men, and who must furiously cultivate their fitness to survive. That such a philosophy of survival, fit for the world of tigers, cannot but bring a fatal catastrophe in the human world, they do not see. They become violently angry at those who protest against it, fearing that such a protest might weaken in them the animal that should be allowed to survive for eternity. Doctors know that infusion of animal blood into human veins does not give vigour to man but produces death, and the intrusion of the animal into humanity will never be for its survival. But faith in man is weakening even in the East; for we have seen that science has enabled the inhuman to prosper, the lie to thrive, the machine to rule in the place of *Dharma*. Therefore in order to save us from the anarchy of weak faith we must stand up to-day and judge the West. But we must guard against antipathy that produces blindness. We must not disable ourselves from receiving truth. For the West has appeared before the present-day world not only with her dynamite of passion and cargo of things but with her gift of truth. Until we fully accept it in a right spirit we shall never even discover what is true in our own civilization and make it generously fruitful by offering it to the world. But it is difficult for us to acknowledge the best in the western civilization and accept it, when we are humiliated. This has been the reason why the West has not yet come to our heart, why we struggle to repudiate her culture because we are under the dark shadow of a western dominance. We need freedom, we need a generous vigour of receptivity which the sense of self-respect can give to us, and then only the mission that Europe has brought to the world will find its fulfilment in our people, and India will also proudly join in the federation of minds in the present age of enlightenment.

"Let us, the dreamers of the East and the West, keep our faith firm in the Life that creates and not in the Machine that constructs—in the power that hides its force and blossoms in beauty, and not in the power that bares its arms and chuckles at its capacity to make itself obnoxious. Let us know that the Machine is good when it helps, but not so when it exploits life; that Science is great when it destroys evil, but not when the two enter into unholy alliance. I believe in the individuals in the West; for on no account can I afford to lose my faith in Man. They also dream, they love, they intensely feel pain and shame at the unholy rites of demon worship that tax the whole world for their supply of bleeding hearts. In the life of these individuals will be wedded East and West; their lamps of sacrifice will burn through the stormy night along the great pilgrim tract of the future, when the names of the statesmen who tighten their noose round the necks of the foreign races will be derided, and the triumphal tower of skulls heaped up in memory of war-lords will have crumbled into dust."

APPENDIX III

MAHATMA GANDHI'S LETTERS TO ENGLISHMEN

LETTER I

"DEAR FRIEND,

"I wish that every Englishman may see this appeal, and give thoughtful attention to it.

"Let me introduce myself to you. In my humble opinion no Indian has co-operated with the British Government more than I have for an unbroken period of twenty-nine years of public life in the face of circumstances that might well have turned any other man into a rebel. I ask you to believe me when I tell you that my co-operation was not based upon the fear of the punishments provided by your laws or any other selfish motives. It was free and voluntary co-operation, based on the belief that the sum-total of the British Government was for the benefit of India. I put my life in peril four times for the sake of the Empire; at the time of the Boer War, when I was in charge of the Ambulance Corps whose work was mentioned in General Buller's despatches; at the time of the Zulu Revolt in Natal, when I was in charge of a similar corps; at the time of the commencement of the late

War, when I raised an ambulance corps, and as a result of the strenuous training had a severe attack of pleurisy; and, lastly, in fulfilment of my promise to Lord Chelmsford at the War Conference in Delhi, I threw myself in such an active recruiting campaign in Khaira District, involving long and trying marches, that I had an attack of dysentery which proved almost fatal. I did all this in the full belief that acts such as mine must gain for my country an equal status in the Empire. So last December I pleaded hard for a trustful co-operation. I fully believed that Mr. Lloyd George would redeem his promise to the Musalmans, and that the revelations of the official atrocities in the Punjab would secure full reparation for the Punjabis. But the treachery of Mr. Lloyd George and its appreciation by you, and the condonation of the Punjab atrocities, have completely shattered my faith in the good intentions of the Government and the nation which is supporting it.

"But, though my faith in your good intentions is gone, I recognize your bravery; and I know that what you will not yield to justice and reason you will gladly yield to bravery.

"See what the British Empire means to India:—

"(1) Exploitation of India's resources for the benefit of Great Britain.

"(2) An ever-increasing military expenditure and a Civil Service the most expensive in the world.

"(3) Extravagant working of every Department in utter disregard of India's poverty.

"(4) Disarmament and therefore emasculation of a whole nation lest an armed nation might imperil the lives of a handful of you in our midst.

"(5) Traffic in intoxicating drugs and liquors for the purpose of maintaining a top-heavy administration.

"(6) Progressively repressive legislation in order to suppress an ever-growing agitation seeking to express a nation's agony.

"(7) Degrading treatment of Indians residing in British Dominions.

"(8) Total disregard of our feelings by glorifying the Punjab Administration and flouting the Muhammadan sentiment.

"I know you would not mind if we could fight and wrest the sceptre from your hands. You know we are powerless to do that; for you have ensured our incapacity to fight in open and honourable battle. Bravery on the battlefield is thus impossible for us. Bravery of the soul still remains open to us."

LETTER II

"DEAR FRIEND,

"I cannot prove my honesty to you if you do not feel it. Some of my Indian friends charge me with camouflage when I say that we need *not* hate Englishmen while we *may* hate the system that they have established. I am trying to show them that one may detest the wickedness of a brother without hating him. Jesus denounced the wickedness of the Scribes and Pharisees, but he did not hate them. He did not enunciate this law of love for the man and hate for the evil in man for himself only, but he taught the doctrines for universal practice. Indeed, I find it in all the Scriptures of the world.

"I claim to be a fairly accurate student of human nature and vivisector of my own failings. I have discovered that man is superior to the system he propounds. And so I feel that you as an individual are infinitely better than the system you have evolved as a corporation. Each one of my countrymen in Amritsar on that fateful April 10th was better than the crowd of which he was a member. He as a man would have declined to kill those innocent bank-managers. But in that crowd many a man forgot himself. Hence it is that an Englishman in office is different from an Englishman outside. Similarly an Englishman in India is different from an Englishman in England. Here in India you belong to a system that is vile beyond description. It is possible, therefore, for me to condemn the system in the strongest terms, without considering you to be bad and without imputing bad motives to every Englishman. You are as much slaves of the system as we are. I want you, therefore, to reciprocate, and not to impute to me motives which you cannot read in the written word. I give you the whole of my motive when I tell you that I am impatient to mend or end a system which has made India subservient to a handful of you, and which has made Englishmen feel secure only in the shadow of the forts and the guns that obtrude themselves on one's notice in India. It is a degrading spectacle for you and for us. Our corporate life is based on mutual distrust and fear. This, you will admit, is unmanly. A system that is responsible for such a state of things is necessarily Satanic. You should be able to live in India as an integral part of its people, and not always as foreign exploiters. One thousand Indian lives against one English life is a doctrine of dark despair, and yet, believe me, it was enunciated in 1919 by the highest of you in the land.

"I almost feel tempted to invite you to join me in destroying a system that has dragged both you and us down. But I feel that I cannot as yet do so. We have not shown ourselves earnest, self-sacrificing, and self-restrained enough for that consummation.

"But I do ask you to help us in the boycott of foreign cloth and in the anti-drink campaign. The Lancashire cloth, as English historians have shown, was forced upon India, and her own world-famed manufacturers were deliberately and systematically ruined. India is therefore at the mercy, not only of Lancashire, but also of Japan, France, and America. Just see what this has meant to India. We send out of India every year sixty crores (more or less) of rupees for cloth. We grow enough cotton for our own cloth. Is it not madness to send cotton outside India, and have it manufactured into cloth there and shipped to us? Was it right to reduce India to such a helpless state?

"A hundred and fifty years ago we manufactured all our cloth. Our women spun fine yarn in their own cottages, and supplemented the earnings of their husbands. The village weavers wove that yarn. It was an indispensable part of national economy in a vast agricultural country like ours. It enabled us in a most natural manner to utilize our leisure. To-day our women have lost the cunning of their hands, and the enforced idleness of millions has impoverished the land. Many weavers have become sweepers. Some have taken to the profession of hired soldiers. Half the race of artistic weavers has died out, and the other half is weaving imported foreign yarn for want of finer hand-spun yarn.

"You will perhaps now understand what boycott of foreign cloth means to India. It is not devised as a punishment. If the Government were to-day to redress the Khilafat and the Punjab wrongs, and consent to India attaining immediate Swaraj, the boycott movement must still continue. Swaraj means at the least the power to conserve Indian industries that are vital to the economic existence of the nation, and to prohibit such imports as may interfere with such existence. Agriculture and hand-spinning are the two lungs of the national body. They must be protected against consumption at any cost.

"This matter does not admit of any waiting. The interests of the foreign manufacturers and the Indian importers cannot be considered, when the whole nation is starving for want of a large productive occupation ancillary to agriculture.

"You will not mistake this for a movement of general boycott of foreign goods. India does not wish to shut herself out of international commerce. Things other than cloth which can be made better outside India, she must gratefully receive upon terms advantageous to the contracting parties. Nothing can be forced upon her. But I do not wish to peep into the future. I am certainly hoping that before long it will be possible for England to co-operate with India on equal terms. Then will be the time for examining trade relations. For the time being I bespeak your help in bringing about a boycott of foreign cloth.

"Of similar and equal importance is the campaign against drink. The liquor shops are an insufferable curse imposed on society. There was never so much awakening among the people as now upon this question. I admit that here the Indian ministers can help more than you can. But I would like you to speak out your mind clearly on that question. Under every system of Government, as far as I can see, prohibition will be insisted on by the Nation. You can assist the growth of the ever-rising agitation by throwing the weight of your influence on the side of the Nation."

Mr. Gandhi made a third appeal, through an interview, which he afterwards published:—

"My attitude", he said, "towards the English is one of utter friendliness and respect. I claim to be their friend, because it is contrary to my nature to distrust a single human being or to believe that any nation on earth is incapable of redemption. I have respect for Englishmen, because I recognize their bravery, their spirit of sacrifice for what they believe to be good for themselves, their cohesion, and their powers of vast organization. My hope about them is that they will at no distant date retrace their steps, revise their policy of exploitation of undisciplined and ill-organized races, and give tangible proof that India is an equal friend and partner in the British Commonwealth to come.

"Whether such an event will ever come to pass will largely depend upon our own conduct. That is to say, I have hope of England because I have hope of India. We shall not for ever remain disorganized and imitative. Beneath the present disorganization, demoralization, and lack of initiative I can discover organization, moral strength, and initiative forming themselves. A time is coming when England will be glad of India's friendship, and India will disdain to reject the proffered hand because it has once despoiled her. I know that I have nothing to offer in proof of my hope. It is based on an immutable faith. And it is a poor faith that is based on proof commonly so-called."

APPENDIX IV

MAHATMA GANDHI'S LETTER TO THE VICEROY

The following is the full text of Mr. Gandhi's letter which he wrote to the Viceroy before beginning his civil disobedience:—

"DEAR FRIEND,

"Now before embarking on civil disobedience and taking a risk I have dreaded to take all these years, I would fain approach you and find a way out. My personal faith is absolutely clear. I cannot intentionally hurt anything that lives, much less fellow human beings, even though they may do the greatest wrong to me and mine. While, therefore, I hold the British rule to be a curse, I do not intend to harm a single Englishman or any legitimate interest he may have in India. I must not be misunderstood. Though I hold British rule in India to be a curse, I do not, therefore, consider Englishmen in general to be worse than any other people on earth. I have the privilege of claiming many Englishmen as my dearest friends. Indeed, much that I have learnt of the evil of British rule is due to the writings of frank and courageous Englishmen who have not hesitated to tell the unpalatable truth about that rule.

"And why do I regard British rule as a curse? It has impoverished the dumb millions by a system of progressive exploitation and by the ruinously expensive military and civil administration which the country can never afford. It has reduced us politically to serfdom. It has sapped the foundations of our culture and by the policy of disarmament it has degraded us spiritually. Lacking inward strength, we have been reduced by all but universal disarmament to a state bordering on cowardly helplessness.

"In common with many of my countrymen I had hugged the fond hope that the proposed Round Table Conference might furnish a solution, but when you said plainly that you could not give any assurance that you or the British Cabinet would pledge yourselves to support a scheme of full dominion status, the Round Table Conference could not possibly furnish the solution for which vocal India is consciously, and the dumb millions unconsciously, thirsting. Needless to say there never was any question of Parliament's verdict being anticipated. Instances are not wanting of the British Cabinet, in anticipation of a parliamentary verdict, having pledged itself to a particular policy. The Delhi interview having miscarried, there was no option for Pandit Motilal Nehru and me but to take steps to carry out the solemn resolution of the Congress arrived at in Calcutta at its session of 1928.

"But the resolution of independence should cause no alarm if the word 'dominion status' mentioned in your announcement has been used in its accepted sense; for, has it not been admitted by responsible British statesmen that dominion status is a virtual independence? What, however, I fear, is that there never has been any intention of granting such dominion status to India in the immediate future. But this is all past history. Since the announcement many events have happened which show unmistakably the trend of British policy. It seems as clear as daylight that responsible British statesmen do not contemplate any alteration in British policy that might adversely affect Britain's commerce with India or require impartial and close scrutiny of Britain's transactions with India.

"If nothing is done to end the process of exploitation, India must be bled with ever-increasing speed. The Finance Member regards as a settled fact that 1s. 6d. ratio which by a stroke of the pen drains India of a few crores, and when a serious attempt is being made, through a civil form of direct action to unsettle this fact, among many others, even you cannot help appealing to the wealthy landed classes to help you to crush that attempt in the name of the order that grinds India to atoms. Unless those who work in the name of the nation understand and keep before all concerned the motive that lies behind the craving for independence, there is every danger of independence itself coming to us so charged as to be of no value to those toiling, voiceless millions for whom it is sought, and for whom it is worth taking. It is for that reason that I have been recently telling the public what independence should really mean. Let me put before you some of the salient points.

"The terrific pressure of land revenue which furnishes a large part of the total revenue must undergo considerable modification in independent India. Even the much-vaunted permanent settlement benefits of a few rich Zemindars, not Ryots. The Ryot has remained as helpless as ever. He is a mere tenant at will. Not only, then, has land revenue to be considerably reduced, but the whole revenue system has to be so revised as to make the Ryot's good its primary concern. But the British system seems to be designed to crush the very life out of him. Even the salt he must use to live is so taxed as to make the burden fall heaviest on him if only because of the heartless impartiality of its incidence. The tax shows itself still more burdensome on the poor man when it is remembered that salt is the one thing he must eat more than the rich men both individually and collectively. The drink and drug revenue too is derived from the poor. It saps the foundations both of their health and their morals. It is defended under the false plea of individual freedom. But in reality it is maintained for its own sake. The ingenuity of the authors of the Reforms of 1919 transferred this revenue to the so-called responsible part of Dyarchy so as to throw the burden of prohibition on it, thus from the beginning rendering it powerless for good. If the unhappy minister wipes out this revenue, he might starve education since in the existing circumstances he has no new source of replacing that revenue. If the weight of taxation has crushed the poor from above, the destruction of the central supplementary industry, i.e. hand-spinning, has undermined their capacity for producing wealth.

"The tale of India's ruination is not complete without a reference to the liabilities incurred in her name. Sufficient has been recently said about these in the public Press. It must be the beauty of a free India to subject all liabilities to the strictest investigation and repudiate those that may be adjudged by an impartal tribunal to be unjust and unfair. The iniquities sampled above are maintained in order to carry on a foreign administration, demonstrably the most expensive in the world. Take your own salary. It is over Rs. 21,000 per month, besides many other indirect additions. The British Prime Minister gets £5,000 per year, a little over Rs. 5,400 per month at the present rate of exchange. You are getting over Rs. 700 per day against India's average income of less than

2 annas per day. The Prime Minister gets Rs. 180 per day against Great Britain's average income of nearly 2 rupees a day. Thus you are getting much over five thousand times India's average income. The British Prime Minister is getting only ninety times Britain's average income. On bended knee I ask you to ponder over this phenomenon. I have taken a personal illustration to drive home the painful truth. I have too great a regard for you as a man to wish to hurt your feelings. I know that you do not need the salary you get. Probably the whole of your salary goes for charity. But the system that provides for such an arrangement deserves to be summarily scrapped. What is true of Viceregal salary is generally true of the whole administration. A radical cutting down of revenue therefore depends upon an equally radical reduction in the expenses of the administration. This means a transformation of the scheme of government. This transformation is impossible without independence. Hence in my opinion the spontaneous demonstration of January 26th in which hundreds of thousands of villagers instinctively participated. To them independence means deliverance from a killing weight.

"Not one of the great British political parties, it seems to me, is prepared to give up the Indian spoils to which Great Britain helps herself from day to day often in spite of the unanimous opposition of Indian opinion. Nevertheless, if India is to live as a nation, if slow death by starvation of her people is to stop, some remedy must be found of immediate relief. The proposed conference is certainly not the remedy. It is not a matter of carrying conviction by argument. The matter resolves itself into one of matching of forces. Conviction or no conviction, Great Britain would defend her Indian commerce and interests by all the forces at her command. India must consequently evolve force enough to free herself from that embrace of death.

"It is common knowledge that, however disorganized and for the time being insignificant it may be, the party of violence is gaining ground and making itself felt. Its end is the same as mine, but I am convinced that it cannot bring the desired relief to the dumb millions, and the conviction is growing deeper and deeper in me that nothing but unadulterated non-violence can check the organized violence of the British Government. Many think non-violence is not an active force. My experience, limited though it undoubtedly is, shows non-violence can be an intensely active force. It is my purpose to set in motion that force as well against the organized violent force of British rule as against the unorganized violent force of the growing party of violence. To sit still would be to give rein to both the forces above mentioned. Having unquestioningly an immovable faith in the efficacy of non-violence as I know it, it would be sinful on my part to wait any longer. This non-violence will be expressed through civil disobedience, for the moment confined to the inmates of the Satyagraha Ashram, but ultimately designed to cover all those who choose to join the movement with its obvious limitation. I know in embarking on non-violence I shall be running what might fairly be termed a mad risk, but the victories of truth have never been won without risks, often of the gravest character. The conversion of a nation that has consciously or unconsciously preyed upon another far more numerous, far more ancient, and no less cultured than itself, is worth any amount of risk. I have deliberately used the word conversion. For my ambition is no less than to convert the British people, through non-violence, and thus make them see the wrong they have done to India. I do not seek to harm your people. I want to serve them, even as I want to serve my own.

"When my eyes were opened and I conceived the idea of non-co-operation my object still was to serve them. I employed the same weapon that I have in all humility successfully used against the dearest members of my family. If I have an equal love for your people with mine it will not long remain hidden. It will be acknowledged by them even as the members of my family acknowledged it after they had tried me for several years. If people join me as I expect they will, the sufferings they will undergo unless the British nation sooner retraces its steps, will be enough to melt the stoniest hearts. The plan through civil disobedience will be to combat such evils as I have sampled out. If we want to sever the British connection, it is because of such evils. When they are removed the path becomes easy. Then the way to friendly negotiation will be opened. If British commerce with India is purified of greed you will have no difficulty in recognizing our independence.

"I respectfully invite you, then, to pave the way for the immediate removal of those evils and thus open the way for a real conference between equals interested only in promoting the common good of mankind through voluntary fellowship, and in arranging the terms of mutual help and commerce equally suited to both.

"You have unnecessarily laid stress upon the communal problems that unhappily affect this land. Important though they undoubtedly are for the consideration of any scheme of government, they have little bearing on the greater problems which are above communities and which affect them all equally. But, if you cannot see your way to deal with these evils and my letter makes no appeal to your heart, on the eleventh day of this month I shall proceed with such co-workers of the ashram as I can take to disregard the provisions of the salt laws. I regard this tax to be the most iniquitous of all from the poor man's standpoint. As the independence movement is essentially for the poorest in the land, a beginning will be made with this evil. The wonder is, we have submitted to the cruel monopoly for so long. It is, I know, open to you to frustrate my design by arresting me. I hope there will be tens of thousands ready in a disciplined manner to take up the work after me and in the act of disobeying the Salt Act, lay themselves open to the penalties of the law that should never have disfigured the statute book.

"I have no desire to cause you unnecessary embarrassment or any at all so far as I can help. If you think there is any substance in my letter, and if you will care to discuss matters with me and if to that end you would like me to postpone the publication of this letter, I shall gladly refrain on receipt of a telegram to that effect soon after this reaches you. You will, however, do me the favour not to deflect me from my course unless you can see your way to conform to the substance of this letter. This letter is not in any way intended as a threat, but is a simple and sacred duty peremptory on the civil resister. Therefore, I am having it specially delivered by a young English friend who believes in the Indian cause and is a full believer in non-violence and whom Providence seems to have sent to me as it were for this very purpose."

APPENDIX V

MAHADEV DESAI'S STORY

The following narrative was told by Miss Slade (Mirabehn) concerning Mahatma Gandhi's secretary, Mahadev Desai, whom she visited in prison, after his arrest as a passive resister:—

> "And now Mahadev arrived. A little pale and worn-looking, but full of spirit and good humour. After some talk he turned to me. 'There is an incident', he said, 'which occurred on my way to jail, which I must tell you about.
>
> " 'The trial was over, and I was put into the prison van. On the back of the van was an English sergeant. There was a huge crowd all round. Suddenly a stone was thrown from somewhere, and it hit the sergeant on the chin, giving him a nasty cut. "Ugh!" exclaimed the man, catching the stone as it fell from his face. "See what your wretched people do! If they stuck to non-violence we could have nothing to say. But look at this behaviour! People who can't be non-violent had better keep out of this movement, or they will soon spoil it." I hastily expressed my sorrow,' continued Mahadev, 'and told him that if he would stop the van, I would speak to the crowds and make them thoroughly ashamed of themselves. "No, I can't

stop the van," said the sergeant—and again he began to complain of the affair. "But what can I do shut up in this van?" I said. "I can only assure you I am extremely pained at the incident, and I would gladly atone for it. Hit me with the stone—it will be good," I added. "No, no!" said the sergeant, beginning to melt. But after a little he again began to get sore on the subject. "Ugh, see what wretched things the people are doing—look at Peshawar—why can't such people keep out of the movement?" "Yes," I replied with deep feeling, and we began to converse about Bapu and the general situation.

" 'But once more he looked at the stone that was in his hand and remarked: "I shall keep this as a memento." "No, please don't do that," I said. "If you have any belief in the sincerity of my sorrow, you will throw it away." This suddenly touched his heart, and then and there he flung it from him!

" 'We were now passing by the Ashram. "See, there's my house," I said, pointing it out to him. "That's nice," he replied, "I have never seen the Ashram. When you come out of prison I must come and visit you." "Yes, do," I said, "I should be delighted. And perhaps now you would give me your name, that I may keep it with me." "Yes, certainly, but I've not got a pencil to write it down with," he remarked. "Here is my pen," I replied, handing it to him through the wire netting. He wrote down his name and was about to hand back the pen through the netting. "No, please keep the pen," I said, "it will be a nice memento, and how much better than the stone!" He was deeply touched, and with appreciation put the little souvenir away in his pocket.

" 'We parted the very best of friends,' concluded Mahadev, his face beaming with delight."

APPENDIX VI

HAROLD LASKI ON THE REPORT

"As a piece of analysis, its finely meshed structure could hardly be bettered. Its argument is closely knit, its logical power superb. Everything is there save an understanding of the Indian mind. Nationalism gets a polite paragraph at the end, written as a half-dubious peroration. Gandhi, who has set half India aflame with new dreams, is dismissed as an administrative incident of which the significance is never seen. You cannot deal with the hopes of a people as though they were studies in logic."

Daily Herald, July 19, 1930.

APPENDIX VII

WALT WHITMAN'S POEM ON LOVE OF COMRADES

The following poem by Walt Whitman is referred to in the closing words of this chapter:—

"I hear it was charged against me that I sought to destroy institutions,
But really I am neither for nor against institutions,
(What indeed have I in common with them? or what with the destruction of them?)
Only I will establish in the Mannahatta and in every city of these States inland and seaboard,
And in the fields and woods, and above every keel little or large that dents the water,
Without edifices or rules or any argument,
The institution of the dear love of comrades."

INDEX

Africa, South, 28
Ahimsa, 21, 53, etc.
Ahmad Khan, Sir Syed, 129
Ahmed, Nazir, 109
Alexander, Horace, 7
Alexander, Olive, 7
Angell, Norman, 83
Asia, 16, etc.
Assam, 48
Australia, 71

Behar, 46, 47
Bengal, 58
Bentinck, Lord, 127
Birkenhead, Lord, 31, 33, 34, 35, etc.
Bombay, 52
Borodada, 132
Botha, General, 33
Brahmo Samaj, 35
Britain, Great, 23, 24, 25, 28, 29, etc.

Cambridge Mission, 115
Canada, 71
Chandpur, 62
China, 162
Commissioners, Simon, 12, 16, etc.
Cyrenaica, 83

Das, C. R., 58
Delhi, New, 41
Deshbandhu, 58, etc.
Dickens, 132
Duff, Alexander, 127
Dutch, 43
Dyer, General, 141

Egypt, 83
Ellis, Mrs., 17
England, 23, etc.

Franciscan Movement, 43, 44
French, 57
French Revolution, 83
Friends, Society, 159

Gandhi, Mahatma, 9, 11, 12, 13, 15, 19, etc.
Gandhism, 42
Garibaldi, 57
George, Lloyd, 141
Ghose, Arabinda, 17, 129
Gokhale, G. K., 112, 119, etc.
Gujarat, 42, 45, etc.
Gurudeva, 16, 21

Hindus, 33, 49, etc.
Humphreys, Mr., 105

India, 19, 24, 25, 26, etc.
India, Young, 40
Indian Christians, 41, 49, 50, etc.
Indian Social Reformer, 56
Iraq, 149
Irish Free State, 63

Jallianwala Bagh, 137
Juhu, 49

Kasturbai, 49
Kenya, 139, 141
Keshub Chander Sen, 130
Khaira, 168

INDEX

Lajpat Rai, 105
Laski, Harold, 188
Lawrence, Sir H., 71, 125
Lee Commission, 32

Macaulay, 126, 127, etc.
Macdonald, Ramsay, 69
Madras, 61, 74
Mahadev Desai, 186, etc.
Malabar, 101
Milton, 28
Morley, Lord, 95
Muhammadans, 33, etc.

Natarajan, Mr. K., 56
National Congress, 61, 63, etc.
Nazareth, 115
Nehru, Jawaharlal, 55, etc.
Nehru, Motilal, 55

Opposition, Leader of, 66, 67, 69
Orissa, 59, 61, etc.
Osburn, Lieut.-Col., 92, 93, 139
Oxford, 131

Palestine, 83
Prime Minister, 66
Punjab, 169
Purna Swaraj, 21, 53, etc.

Reform Constitution, 81
Ripon, Lord, 112
Roberts, Charles, 96
Roy, Ram Mohan, 127, 128, etc.
Ruhr, 57

Salt Act, 185
Sapru, Sir Tej Bahadur, 14, 85
Sastri, Srinavasa, 85
Saxons, 92
Scotland, 23
Scott, Sir Walter, 132, 133
Seeley, Sir John, 89, 90, etc.
Setalvad, Sir C., 85
Shankarlal Banker, 56
Sholapur, 157
Simla, 71
Simon Commission, 19, 32, etc.
Simon Report, 74, 82, etc.
Simon, Sir John, 32, etc.
Skeen Commission, 32
Smuts, General, 33
Sobhani Umar, 56
Spectator, 42
Syria, 83
Syrian Church, 101

Tagore, Dwarkanath, 127
Tagore, Rabindranath, 14, 19, 21, 153, 159, etc.
Telegraph, Daily, 56
Thompson, Prof. E. J., 129
Tokyo, 14
Tunis, 83

Uriyas, 73, 74

Viceroy, 34, 35, etc.

Walsh, Rt. Rev., 63
Whitehall, 71
Whitman, Walt, 189
Wilson, President, 136

Yeaxlee, Basil, 17
Youth League, 13, etc.

Zaka, Ullah, 109